I0136131

Tragic to Magic

\-

Anger, Anxiety, Depression or Happiness, it's a Choice

ANTHONY GILMOUR

Dwyers Pacific Press Pty Ltd
PO Box 101 Darnum, VIC 3822
Victoria, AUSTRALIA

First Published 2013: Edition 1

This book is copyright. Apart from any fair dealing for the purpose of private study, research, criticism or review as permitted under the Copyright Act. No part of this book may be reproduced, stored in a retrieval system, communicated or transmitted in any form or by any means without prior written permission. All inquiries should be made direct to the author at email: info@wholemindstrategies.com.au

Illustrations and artwork by Anthony Gilmour
Edited by Christopher Roering
Published by Dwyers Pacific Press Pty Ltd

© Whole Mind Strategies Pty Ltd. All rights reserved.

ISBN-13: 978-0-975676288
ISBN-10: 0975676288

Dedicated to my grandson Oaklyn - forever young.

The true strength of human spirit: love, compassion and kindness. It is with us when we need to endure what seems unendurable. And it is found in the heart of man, not the head.

CONTENTS

ACKNOWLEDGMENTS

There are a number of people that I would like to acknowledge. The first and foremost is Christopher Roering. Chris is a book publisher and a psychotherapist. I asked Chris for some feedback after writing the first few chapters, his feedback and editing has turned this book into what it is today and I will be forever in his debt. I have been driven by his positive feedback, enthusiasm and suggestions and admire his intellect, compassion and sense of humour. True friends seem to appear when we need them most. Lessa Wyatt, Kaz Cox, Sophie Jones, Max Baker and Dr Mark Roberts, have also given such positive feedback about the book and I thank them all for their input. Dr Leonie Leivenzon's feedback was much appreciated and resulted in changing many of the ways I presented this information.

My mother and father, children and grandchildren, have all been an inspiration to me and I would also like to acknowledge my wife Julie. Her unconditional love and support over the years has taught me how to be a better man. If there is such a thing as a soul mate then I have truly found mine.

CHAPTER ONE

Introduction

As a psychotherapist, when I see a client for the first time, I listen for the first ten minutes or so and the problem usually becomes apparent. I will then say. 'Let me show you how the mind works; what makes us tick - the roadmap to where you are now and how to get to where you would like to be.' A happy person is living a successful life. This book is the roadmap to living a happy life in a nutshell and you don't need to be a brain surgeon to understand it. It is simple and I like to keep it this way. Understand the structure of what you create through your thoughts, change it and you change the experience. I was almost fifty before I turned to psychotherapy, long enough to sort out the wheat from the chaff, and there is a lot of chaff around!

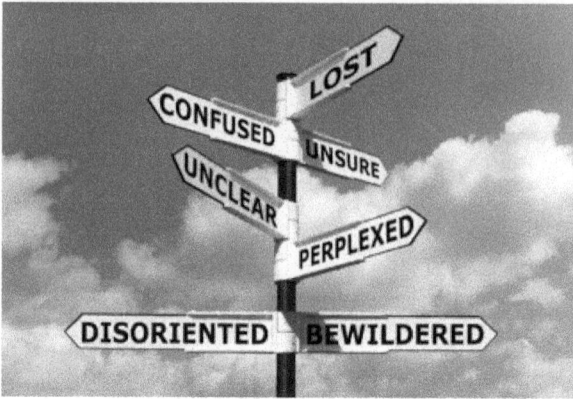

Many years ago I was Managing Director of an engineering company travelling the world on a good salary and with a new car, my own home, a fantastic wife, plus good friends. Some may have seen me as being very successful considering my humble beginnings, but I wasn't happy most of the time. Don't get me wrong here: there is nothing wrong with working hard and having nice things; but it should be the *by-product* of a happy life - not the reason for it. This underlying feeling of unhappiness resulted in my beginning to study self-help books and attending self-help seminars - but to no avail. I was still an unhappy chappie. I even tried a seven day *Date with Destiny* seminar with Anthony Robbins (costing a small fortune). I came out of it feeling that I had changed my life for good, but within a few months I was back to feeling unfulfilled. I came across many seminar junkies looking for the next hit after the previous one had worn off and knew this wasn't for me. 'Why weren't the changes permanent?' I would ask myself while regretting the money I had spent.

At this point I started to study psychology in order to understand myself and my staff better. I studied Sigmund Freud and thought he probably had just as many problems as his clients! Freud's theory of the Oedipus complex (the theory about how a young boy has sexual desires for his mother and jealousy of his father) just seemed plain odd. It made me wonder about Freud's upbringing and underlying

2

thoughts. I have no recollection of ever being attracted to my mother or jealous of my father. Freud's treatment of his associate Carl Jung, who didn't follow his point of view in many ways, confirmed to me that Freud had his own demons. He did however introduce me to the subconscious mind, and I acknowledge the great leap forward in psychotherapy as a result of his work.

There were many others to study, like Carl Rogers and Viktor Frankle, and I found a great deal of common sense when reading William Glasser in his work on reality therapy and choice theory. In a bid to gain more knowledge I looked at how views in psychology fitted with the teachings of Christ and Buddha. For example the teachings of Lester Levenson, the creator of the *Sedona Method*, developed later by Hale Dwoskin that were similar to the Buddha's teachings in so many ways.

Now, let's take a look at how we gain knowledge. Stage one, you can be told something or read it. Stage two, you can intellectually understand it. To get to stage three, the final stage, you need to have proof to really know it: you have to experience it in some way. At that stage in my life I wasn't experiencing it. Why? I came to the conclusion that it was because of the habit patterns in my mind.

The mind is brilliant. We teach it through repetition to drive a car and then the subconscious mind takes over and drives the car without the driver even thinking about it. He or she is then free to think about what they will have for dinner when they get home. Meanwhile the car is blissfully driven along with the subconscious at the wheel and keeping an eye out for any threats. The driver is not even conscious of driving. It just happens on auto pilot. Our subconscious is a perfect servant once trained and is usually a better driver than the conscious mind! Try to consciously stay in the middle of your lane when driving and you will see what I mean. This is the brilliance of the mind and also the reason why it is so difficult to change it. Try driving in a country where they drive on the opposite side of the road for the first time. It's guaranteed to make the heart skip a beat or two. This is the reason all the books and seminars didn't work for me. The mind reverted back to its old patterns.

This book is designed to offer the first and second stages of knowledge - the intellectual understanding of how the mind works and how we create the way we feel. Don't believe anything I say in this book without testing it yourself. Only then will you have the third stage - the experience of it, the proof of it and ultimately true knowledge.

So how do we define a successful person? From a psychological point of view, a successful person is a happy person. When we are not happy it is usually because we are postponing our happiness to a time when we might get something we feel we are lacking now. But more about that later....

'From Tragic to Magic' is a compilation of the tools I use to help clients in my psychotherapy practice. It could just as easily have been called *the psychology of happiness* or *the psychology of success*. A happy person is a successful person. I hope you enjoy your journey through these pages.

CHAPTER TWO

Understanding Habits, Needs and Negative Emotions

It had been eight years earlier that I had left the fair shores of England by boat, I was twenty one years of age. I had headed for Australia looking for adventure and a new life. And now here I was back for a holiday in Maryport, the place of my birth. I was standing in the Labour Club with a pint of beer in one hand and a set of darts in the other. The three darts thudded into the dartboard. The chalk was moving on the chalkboard as soon as the last arrow hit the dartboard. In less than three seconds, the total was added together and then subtracted from the figure on the chalkboard. It had been calculated by David, one my best friends from childhood, and I stood in awe of this human calculator.

David and I had grown up together living just around the corner from each other. We played football on the local field most summer nights and built bonfires together in winter. During our school holidays we would head off on long adventurous treks across the countryside. We would meander through woods and forests or stroll along the sea front. We would often lie on our backs and chew grass while we watched the clouds drifting across the sky. We talked about what we would like to do when we grew up to be men. The one thing David didn't do was spend much time at school. We would head off to school together but I would often arrive alone. David would choose to left turn at Dolby's Chemist shop. This turn would take him into town while the rest of us headed down the long road to school. A part of me envied his ability to make that choice, as I was too afraid of the repercussions should I be found out. David wasn't that interested in school. Even when we started school at the age of five I remember him sleeping beside me with his head on the desk at the back of the class. And now here he was, faster than a calculator when it came to calculating the scores at darts.

So how can someone who was not very good at, or interested in maths at school become this human calculator, calculating at super-human speed? It's all about repetition, and the development of habits through repetition.

Repetition is the mother of skill, and skill is the result of habit. This is the brilliance of the mind. We teach the subconscious mind to do something and then it does it automatically, without thinking. We train the subconscious and it becomes our perfect servant. Compare a new born child's abilities with your own. Adults walk, talk, get dressed and make coffee without much conscious thought. We might consciously make the decision to do something, but then most of it is done subconsciously.

We are taught to do many things in life - riding bikes, using computers, driving cars, playing football or netball - even how to dress and brush our teeth. But no one teaches us anything about our minds and how we use our amazing minds to create our lives. I find this strange. We have the most amazing computer in the universe between our ears and no one has taught us how to use it. And to make matters worse, much of the programming is done by others before we have developed a rational logical faculty of mind. The people in charge of this programming usually have absolutely no idea how it works. We develop sporting programs to develop physical fitness and skills, but there is not much around to teach people how the mind works or how to develop mental fitness for life. Much of this book comes from programs I have used with clients - programs that have proven over the past ten years to be effective. But don't take it on face value - test it for yourself!

The way we feel is usually a result of our automatic mental habits of thinking - the way we have trained our brains to see the world. If we understand how our brains are trained then surely we can choose what we train them? First, we need to understand what drives our behaviour.

Our behaviour is like the wheels of a car. The ways we think and act are the front wheels leading forward and the way we feel and our physiology are the back wheels following. The engine driving it all contains our five genetic human needs. Our need for love and connection; for empowerment (a feeling that we are important to people: that we have an influence on our lives); for freedom; for fun; and for survival. Survival isn't normally a problem if we have our health, food, shelter and freedom from harm. Freedom and fun go out of the window when the needs for love, connection and empowerment are not being met. Our needs for love and connection and empowerment are usually met through our relationships with others. I would suggest that over ninety five per cent of our problems are relationship problems – past, present, or lack of. I have found this to be true in my practice as a psychotherapist.

These five needs come in different strengths that create different personalities. The person with a high need for love and connection would usually like to be around others most of the time - a sociable person. The person with a high need for empowerment needs to feel important to others and have an influence over their lives - they usually like their own lives to be organised and structured. Someone with a high need for freedom might like their own space; they don't need to be around others all the time. The person with a high need for fun might like new and interesting things and being spontaneous. The person with a high need for survival would tend to be more cautious and less spontaneous. All these needs in differing strengths create a myriad of differing personalities.

My wife has a high need for love and connection - a very sociable person who likes parties and being around others. I on the other hand have a high need for freedom and fun. I have skydived and done scuba diving, but these days I tend to meditate, read books and paint. I like my own space. You can see the obvious conflict. My wife likes to be around people most of the time and I like my own space and doing my own thing. We have learned to compromise over the past thirty years of being together. But that wasn't always the way. We had some magnificent *take no prisoner* battles in the early days that we were lucky to survive.

Most of our destructive negative emotions are based on fear - a fear of lacking.

There are basically two types of emotions: love based emotions and fear based emotions. Most of our destructive negative emotions are based on fear - a fear of lacking. I believe that to understand this is to understand what stops us being happy.

If we want to find the root of our negative emotions we need to look a little further. To a distortion of these needs – *wants*.

A need is something basic that must be met for us to be happy. A *want* is a feeling of lacking something we don't necessarily need. An example of this might be 'I *need* healthy food to survive. But I *want* to have donuts and cakes.' Often our short-term wants override our long-term needs.

About 2500 years ago a guy called Buddha told us that all life is suffering. This was the first of his *noble truths*. The second noble truth was that all suffering comes from craving. So where does this craving come from? It comes from wanting something different. By wanting something different you are basically telling yourself that you are not happy now; you are lacking something that stops you from being happy in this moment - *now*. Due to this perceived lack you are looking at the world in a fearful way and this in turn releases the physiology of fear - our flight or fight response. The body reacts with a general discharge from the sympathetic nervous system releasing hormones such as adrenaline, cortisol and noradrenaline. These hormones produce uncomfortable sensations in the body that are designed by nature to protect us. They create a craving for relief from the stressor by causing us to run away from or fight the threat: *The flight of fight response.* Once the threat is resolved we go back to our normal state.

This system has worked well in our evolution to protect us from the physical threat of harm from wild animals such as sabre toothed tigers. It is not working so well for us now from an emotional point of view - from a mind conceiving irrational threats, and these irrational threats are wants. So let's take a look at where these wants arise when looking at the mind of today, and in what way these wants are a distortion of our needs.

We can break down the wants into four basic areas to keep things simple.

Love is not something you can get – only something you can give.

The want for approval

The want for approval is a distortion of the need for love and connection.

Is it possible to get one person's approval all the time? Not likely! Ask my wife. If I could get her approval all the time it would be fantastic, but I am not perfect. I have my faults just like everyone else. Could I get everyone's approval? No, not much chance of that happening.

The fear of public speaking has its roots in the want for approval. The fear that people won't approve of the way you look, what you are saying and how you are saying it. What if I look foolish, make mistakes or start to blush or stutter? Better just to say nothing and keep my head down because I fear I will not be approved of.

The more you want approval, the more you fear you are lacking it

Social anxiety (a fear of social interaction with others) has its roots in the want for approval as do many low self-esteem issues. The more you want approval, the more you fear you are lacking it. It is impossible to get one person's approval all the time and it is impossible to get everyone's approval. Let's face it; some people are just not going to like us. It's just a fact of life. And yet we crave for people to say nice things about us and have an aversion to them saying things we don't like. 'If people say nice things about me I will feel loved.' Not really. You will just feel approved of and crave more of the same. *You see, love is not something you can get - it is only something you can give.* When a child is born the parents usually have an overwhelming feeling of love for this innocent little baby. The baby is looking back wondering what the hell these strange looking gushing things are. It's the love the parents feel for the child that makes them feel good - not the love the child gives back.

The more you want approval, the more you must feel you lack it. And your mind sees this lack as a threat.

Anger and frustration have their roots in the want to control.

The want for control

The want for control is a distortion of the need for empowerment.

Empowerment is to have an influence over things in your life. This need for empowerment is often distorted into wanting to control things. You can't even control your body as it ages. You can't control another person as most parents find out with regard to their children. Control is just an illusion. It's like a want for certainty, but nothing is certain. Anger and frustration have their roots in the want to control. Let's just take the example of a person not being happy because it's wet, cold and raining outside. You can't control the weather. It just is. Not good or bad. It just is. We create a judgement that it is bad for us by wanting it to be warm and sunny but we can't control the weather. It simply just is. You might have a preference for something else, but if you can't have an influence over it, what's the point of losing your happiness over it? How many times do we get frustrated over things beyond our influence - such as being stuck in traffic? Or when our football team loses, or when we get a flat tyre? When the golf ball won't go where we want it to go, or when others don't behave the way we would like them to? The want for control can be seen in the way some people seek to have power over others. Many wars have been fought because of this want. We try to control nature but we soon learn the lesson. The power of nature is far beyond our control. Volcanos spew forth their ash and lava, and tsunamis, cyclones and hurricanes destroy towns and cities.

Nothing is permanent – nothing is secure.

The want for security

The want for security is a distortion of the need for survival. How can anything be secure when nothing is permanent? We want security of relationships and yet we all die. No relationship is permanent. Security of assets, income and jobs are not permanent. Money comes and goes. Jobs are lost. Assets rust away or are soon past their use by date. Everything is arising and passing away in a universe where everything is constantly changing and nothing is permanent. Even the sun will one day exhaust its energy and eventually its light will go out. Nothing for me to worry about though; I won't be around that long because my physical existence is not permanent. Just take a look around and see for yourself. Most of the older cars have already gone and the computer that I type this on has already replaced my old one just a few months ago and it will be replaced in times to come. Everything I see around me in the room where I sit will one day find its way to the tip.

Many addictions are formed by the want to escape.

The want to escape

The want to escape is a distortion of the need for freedom and fun. It usually rears its head because we are stuck in the other wants; approval, control and security. Suicide is the ultimate want to escape. It is the want to escape the current situation or responsibilities in life. You can't escape the ups and downs, or the twists and turns of life. It's a roller coaster ride - not a flat road. Many addictions are formed by the want to escape. People turn to drugs, drink, food or even gambling to escape the way they feel about what is happening, or not happening in their lives. They want to escape not being happy. If you are sitting at work watching the clock and wishing you were somewhere else, this is the want to escape. You have responsibilities and need to work, but you would rather be out playing golf.

You can't escape the responsibilities of living or of being a parent or partner in a relationship. Responsibility is just our ability to respond. It is our ability to make a choice but sometimes we feel there is no other choice but to try to escape the situation - to run away. You can't run away from life. Everything is changing and nothing is permanent. Even a situation where a person has thoughts of suicide is in most cases a situation that will pass and resolve itself if that person stays the course. The want to escape comes from a feeling of hopelessness. This is the flight part of our *flight or fight* response. When you want to escape, you are not focusing on solutions because, in a mind filled with fear, escape is the only solution. There is nothing wrong with wanting to escape a physical threat, it's our natural instinct. The want to escape an emotional threat is another thing. The needs for freedom and fun are frustrated when we feel disconnected and disempowered. This is when the want to escape usually pops its head up. Why would you want to escape this moment, when this is the only time you really have? The want to escape is the want for something different to what you have now. Drugs, alcohol, food and gambling are just short term escapes. The problems are still there when you get back – and usually with added consequences.

Food, shelter and freedom from harm are all we need to survive.

This moment is the only time we really have.

The happiest person I have met is a guy called Kevin. Kevin worked on a radial arm drill at an engineering company where I once worked. We used to joke that Kevin was the happiest guy we knew because he wasn't married. We knew the perils of upsetting the once shy young ladies we had married. Those same young women had now taken on the disapproving looks and lectures our mothers used to give us when we didn't quite behave the way they wanted. (Let's face it; men often take a lot longer than women to settle into the responsibilities of being married and rearing a family.)

Kevin was your typical old style Aussie guy aged in his mid-fifties - old slouch hat tipped to one side, checked shirt with sleeves rolled up and a thick leather belt holding up his green work pants. Kevin always had a smile and something to say to everyone who walked past. He would call out 'Hello gorgeous' to the office women as they walked past to make them feel good and everyone liked him. You couldn't avoid it: his happiness was infectious!

I mentioned to him one day that his mates thought he was happy all the time because he wasn't married. He laughed and said that he had a 'lady friend'. He saw her a few days each week and had done so for many years, but they didn't feel the need to change this arrangement when it worked so well for both of them. I asked Kevin why he seemed happy all the time and this is what he told me:

Kevin had a best friend all the way through school and he said they were like brothers. They did everything together, played football and even supported the same football team. One day they were supposed to be going to the football together and Kevin went to his friend's house to pick him up, but his friend hadn't woken up. Kevin's best friend had died in his sleep. Kevin said he couldn't believe it. His friend had been one of the fittest guys he knew. Then he looked me in the eyes and said: 'You never know when your time is up. So every day I wake up I am just glad to still be here. If I wake up in the morning then everything else is a bonus. And if it's my last day I'm not going to waste it bothering about rubbish.'

I asked him if he got bored on the drill doing the same thing day after day, and his reply was this: 'A job worth doing is worth doing well. You can be happy washing dishes if you are just doing what needs to be done. Some of the people who work here don't want to be here. They would rather be playing golf or down at the pub instead of just doing what needs to be done. What's the point of wanting to be somewhere else when this is where you are? That's just plain silly - It just makes the clock go slower when you watch it.'

This is the gospel according to Kevin; a very simple way of looking at life. Was Kevin successful? If success is the attainment of a worthy goal, then the highest goal of all is to be happy. All other goals are just steps along the path to try to reach this ultimate goal. All goals we undertake are designed to seek pleasure and avoid pain – the pleasure we seek is happiness.

If we look at the Buddha's teaching, he talks about the impermanence of things. We cling to the good things and feelings and have an aversion to the things and feelings we don't like. Yet they will all arise and pass away. It is also interesting to note that neurological testing on some

Buddhist monks has shown them to be among the happiest people. I find this very interesting as they have virtually no possessions of note. They focus on love and compassion for all living things and let go of craving. They meet their basic human needs through co-operation and contribution. We can now look back at my old friend Kevin's philosophy of life to see him embrace his own impermanence in much the same way a Buddhist monk might.

I am not suggesting we all need to become monks, meditating in caves to be happy. Kevin didn't. But there are some very basic lessons we can learn, as we walk through this journey of life, that can enrich our lives and make them much more enjoyable. Too often we postpone our happiness until a time when we get something we want. It stops us enjoying the moment now and yet this moment is all we have. The past is gone and the future is yet to arrive. This moment is the only time we really have. All time outside of this moment is psychologically mind created time and it only exists in our minds.

CHAPTER THREE

The Formation of Many Beliefs

What you believe is what you see

The old saying *'seeing is believing'* is the wrong way around. What we believe is what we see. So where do much of our beliefs come from? Most of our beliefs about ourselves, our lives and others come from the way others relate to us and communicate with us. Many of these beliefs are formed at an early age long before we have developed a rational and logical mind. Children tend to believe what they are told. They believe in Father Christmas, the Tooth Fairy and the Easter Bunny. If you tell them they are stupid, they will believe that too.

William Glasser's *'choice theory'* and in particular, the habits of communication can give us some insights into the formation of many of our positive and negative beliefs. Glasser's theory of the connecting and disconnecting habits of communication were a revelation to me.

The seven connecting habits are:

Caring, supporting, trusting, encouraging, befriending, listening and negotiating (instead of telling).

The more we support and encourage a child, the more that child will grow. There is no limit to the positive beliefs formed through these connecting habits. Most good parents use these connecting habits without thinking. These are the habits we use with our best friends - the only habits we use on our best friends - which is why we feel connected and empowered by them and like to be around them. But how many times do we withdraw these connecting habits when our children don't behave the way we would like them to? Far too often I'm afraid. What happens when we withdraw these connecting habits? The child feels unloved, unworthy and not approved of. Negative limiting beliefs begin to form or are reinforced.

When people use connecting habits on us we feel connected and empowered. I have also found that when using connecting habits, I meet my own needs for love and connection. It works both ways. When they are used on us as children, we feel loved, approved of and liked. Through this (especially when we are children) we form positive unlimited beliefs about ourselves and others. Our positive self-esteem grows.

I have to admit that my parenting skills were lacking. I also recognise that this was apparent in my skills as a manager of others at work. I see my life as a process of evolution, so I don't expect to be perfect. When the student is ready the teacher will appear. In my case the teacher was William Glasser and what he taught seemed like common sense. But common sense is not that common!

There are also disconnecting habits, and even the best of parents have used these on their children.

The seven disconnecting habits are:

Criticising, complaining, nagging, blaming, threatening, punishing, bribing.

Even the best of parents will have used these disconnecting habits at some time on their children. A great number of bosses use these disconnecting habits on their staff. It's the way people bully each other. These are the habits we use to control someone (although they only serve to make the other person feel disconnected and disempowered). The interesting thing about these habits is that the person using them must feel disconnected and disempowered to be using them in the first place.

Bullies feel disconnected and disempowered.

Disconnecting habits are like a double edged sword. These habits cut the person they are used on and cut the user. What we can see emerging from this is the want for control we discussed before. The more you want control the more you feel you lack it. Disconnecting habits usually come from a place of anger or frustration. If these habits are used on a child and they will feel unloved, unworthy and not liked. Tell a child they are stupid often enough and the child will start to believe it. And what we believe is what we see. A child might have the same brain as Albert Einstein but they no longer use it. We tend to take the disconnecting habits personally without realising that it isn't personal. It's the other person who has the problem because they want to control us.

You can manage resources but you lead people.

We can see these connecting and disconnecting habits at work in many areas. They are also evident in our parenting style at home, for example, or in a child's interaction with others at school - or in how we communicate with others in sporting teams or in the workforce. But let's use the example of this in the workforce. For want of a better description, we will call the different styles of managers lead managers, and boss managers. You see, you can manage resources but you lead people.

Lead Managers

Lead Managers will connect with and empower staff through positive feedback and connecting habits. They see mistakes as opportunities to learn; they build morale and they know the team creates the results. Staff will enjoy coming to work. They are creative and they take less time off. They feel they belong to a team. Most will feel an obligation to work hard and do well, they focus on their work and solutions. Lead Managers create a culture of positive expectation. This is like putting money in the bank. You create a surplus. You will eventually gain interest on this investment that will be returned to you in kind. Lead Managers have a positive influence on people.

Boss Managers

Boss Managers disconnect and disempower staff through negative feedback or disconnecting habits or no feedback at all. (When talking about boss managers I am talking about the bossy people that use these disconnecting habits all the time on subordinates thinking they are controlling them.) They see mistakes as opportunities to blame. They destroy morale. They think that they are the ones that get the results. Staff don't enjoy being around a boss manager. Many don't enjoy going to work and they may also gossip and complain behind the boss's back. They take more time off work. This results in people being afraid to make mistakes, and so stops creativity. Workers are not focused on work but on problems with their boss. This can creates a culture of fear and stress. This is like taking money out of the bank. You create a deficit and you will have to pay interest on this deficit at some time in the future. The loss of efficiency and even the loss of good employees will result. You can't fully control another, it's false economy.

We can now start to understand the formation of our positive and negative belief system - how our self-esteem is affected through our relationships with others. We start to develop some irrational fears - the wants for approval, control and security - and the world becomes a scary place to live.

I did feel some guilt, regret and disappointment over my own communications skills with my children once I understood the habits of communication. We were never taught how to be parents at school. We usually did what was done to us. And even the best of parents have used disconnecting habits to try to control their children. I see the subconscious mind like an amazing computer that is being programmed by people such as parents, with absolutely no idea what damage they are doing. Luckily, we can reprogram it, and once programed, it becomes a perfect servant. Disconnecting habits are all about control but we can never really control another person. However we can have a positive influence over people by using connecting habits.

Guilt is one of the most ridiculous emotions we can foster.

Parents often use guilt as a method of control, but guilt is one of the most ridiculous emotions we can foster. Guilt offers a lesson and nothing more. You rob a bank, feel guilty, give the money back and never rob another bank. The guilt has served its purpose. I soon got over the guilt in my parenting skills and took the lesson to heart.

I wonder just how often you use disconnecting habits on yourself in your own negative self-talk and how guilty you make yourself feel. We often take over where others left off. You can become your own biggest critic, feeding your own negative self-esteem and negative belief system. You have to be careful about what you keep suggesting to yourself. *Your continued suggestions will become your beliefs and what you believe you will see.*

 ***The new car or bigger house should be the by-product of a happy life, not the reason for it.***

To simplify the belief system I will take an approach that many in psychological circles might not agree with, but I believe in simplifying things.

I group the non-limiting beliefs into the category of the true self - our positive self-esteem. The negative limiting beliefs I refer to, for simplicity, as the ego - our negative self-esteem. I see the ego as a protection mechanism that has developed to protect us from emotional pain, because much of it was created through the emotional pain we felt as a child. When the child thought it was a victim of something or someone, it sought approval, control and security; all the things it felt it lacked at that time in its life. The ego wants us to feel superior, but in the wanting of it, it makes us feel inferior. If we have the approval of others we feel superior. If we have control or power over others we feel superior. If we get money and possessions we feel secure and superior. Any want that is satisfied will soon be replaced by another want - and so the suffering of craving follows us - never satisfied. Don't get me wrong here; there is nothing wrong with having a preference for the new car or bigger house but, it should be a by-product of a happy life, not the reason for it.

If you want sweet plums you don't plant the seeds of a bitter lemon.

I use a technique with clients that you can try. I call this the *time out* technique. I like to make learning something fun. Learning to stop disconnecting habits and use only connecting habits can be fun too. First you need to commit these habits to memory. You can print them on a card and carry it in your wallet or purse. You can also write them on a piece of paper and stick it on the fridge. Read them often. If one person uses the disconnecting habits on the other they just respond by making a 'T' sign with their hands saying '*time out*, are you criticising me? ' (Or whatever the disconnecting habit might be). The other person then has to smile and apologise without argument. I also get them to ask this question to themselves before saying anything. 'Is what I am about to say going to bring us closer together or move us further apart?' If what you are about to say will move you further apart, bite your tongue. If it will only move you further apart and you want to get closer, It isn't worth the grief.

If you want sweet plums you don't plant the seeds of a bitter lemon. What seeds are you planting?

CHAPTER FOUR

How the Mind Works

Our imagination fills in the gaps of perception.

Imagination

We create our reality through our imagination, so what are we creating? So many people create drama in their lives because that's what they imagine through a system of wanting. They see a lack in their lives and are left lacking. What is wrong with seeing this world as a world of adventure and comedy? It is a choice, but the habit patterns of the mind, looking for threats and wants, make it see drama, and so create drama. Do you imagine a fearful world? All too often we don't see the imagination as a tool of creation. Many tools can be dangerous if we don't use them properly.

Imagination

Our imagination is our creative faculty.
It can create good things and bad.

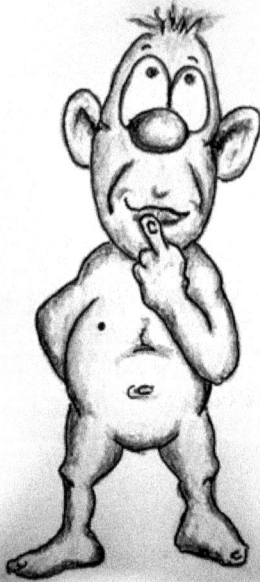

We use our imagination to determine what is
possible and probable.

We often say our imagination runs wild but we can harness it to create the things we would like to bring into our lives. This is where we have choice. *The only thing that stops us believing we have no choice is that we are sometimes stuck in the habit of wanting.*

What is coming in through the senses is just information. The eyes are like cameras, the ears like microphones. Taste and smell are just chemical receptors; the skin like a mass of pressure and heat sensors. The body is an information gathering machine. We take this information and try to give it meaning, and this is where we have a choice. We have a choice how we focus our minds. In our minds, we are often filling in the gaps in sensory information through our imagination to give it meaning. An example of this could be seeing two people whispering, and imagining that they are talking about you. We can choose to focus our mind in a negative way or a positive way. But often the front wheels of the car (the way we think and act) are stuck in a rut, focusing on wants.

The positive unlimited beliefs tap into the true self and the negative limiting beliefs form our protection mechanism, the ego.

Beliefs

Many of our beliefs are created by the way people relate to us, especially when we are children. Do these beliefs of the ego work for us or do they create problems for us? Sadly the negative beliefs strip us of our ability to be happy and to achieve what we would like to bring into our lives. These beliefs are not you. You were not born with them and they are nothing more than irrational fears. The positive unlimited beliefs tap into the true self and the negative limiting beliefs form our protection mechanism, the Ego.

Beliefs

Beliefs are filters of perception
Many beliefs are created through the use of connecting and disconnecting habits

True Self

Positive beliefs

Connecting habits create empowering beliefs and high self esteem.

Ego Self

Negative beliefs

Disconnecting habits create limiting beliefs and low self esteem

Using disconnecting habits in our self talk disconnects and disempowers us.
It reinforces limiting beliefs

We are often so afraid to fail that sometimes we won't even try.

Our own negative self-talk, and the use of disconnecting habits on ourselves, feeds negative beliefs. They continue to grow, self-sabotaging our abilities and achievements. What you believe you will see. And if you believe you will fail, guess what? You will fail. We are often so afraid to fail that sometimes we won't even try. As a child did you fail to walk when you fell after taking that first step; or fell off your bike when you first learned to ride it? You didn't fail: you were learning all the time. Making mistakes is how we learn. We are not perfect - we are in a process of evolving. We are evolving through the mistakes we make, and mistakes are a natural part of our learning process. The belief system becomes a filter in the way we see the world and what we believe we see.

Conscious focus is a choice

To start to train the mind we have to understand that we have a choice in the way we focus our creative ability and reclaim our ability to choose. This can be difficult at first. The negative habits of the mind are habits and the ego is a protection mechanism. The ego doesn't want to relinquish control. If it relinquishes control, how will you be protected? Protected from what? From irrational emotional wants that can never be satisfied? The ego tells us we have a right to be afraid, a right to be upset and a right to be angry. It can be very determined in this. It knows from past experience that we didn't always get what we wanted.

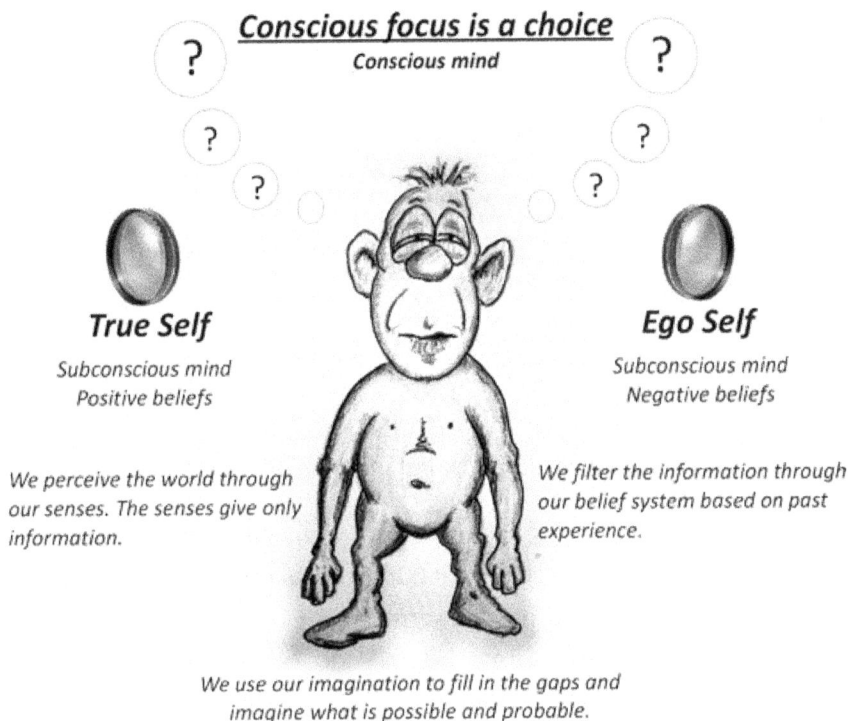

Conscious focus is a choice
Conscious mind

True Self
Subconscious mind
Positive beliefs

Ego Self
Subconscious mind
Negative beliefs

We perceive the world through our senses. The senses give only information.

We filter the information through our belief system based on past experience.

We use our imagination to fill in the gaps and imagine what is possible and probable.

The problem with choosing to change is the habit patterns of the mind. As I mentioned earlier, I liken this to driving down the road on the left hand side in Australia without even thinking about it. Try driving down the right hand side in America and see how uncomfortable it can be. It takes us out of our comfort zone and our comfort zone is the limit of our positive beliefs. So it will be uncomfortable when we first start making these changes - and that's fine. As you expand your comfort zone you are growing and evolving. Our lives should be a continuous process of expanding and evolving. But all too often we find our comfort zones shrinking or contracting.

Shifting your focus from wants to expectations

How do we change the mind from wanting? This should be the question you are asking yourself by now. Well, this shift is subtle. If we look at a want as a fear of lacking something, we can see it is pessimistic, rigid, fearful and focusing on problems. The subtle change is to turn this want into an expectation. Why? Because expectations are more optimistic, flexible and focus on solutions.

A want is never satisfied until we get what we want.

An example of this could be my last client for the day coming in at 8:00pm. I expect to be finished by 9:00pm. If it is 9:15pm that's fine, it's my last client; I can be flexible. If I wanted to be finished by 9:00pm, I would be looking at the clock at 8:55pm. At 9:00pm I would be getting frustrated and by 9:05pm I would be getting very irritated. Now you can see that a want is never satisfied until we get what we want. It's a subtle change in the way we think that creates a big difference in the way we feel. We rob ourselves of our happiness with these little irritations, when it really doesn't matter at all.

From wants to expectations
Conscious choice of mind

? ? ? ? ? ?

True Self
Subconscious mind
Positive beliefs

Expectations
Love
Optimistic
Focus on solutions
Connecting habits
Positive actions

Higher consciousness

Ego Self
Subconscious mind
Negative beliefs

Wants
Fears
Pessimistic
Focus on problems
Disconnecting habits
Negative actions

Flight or fight

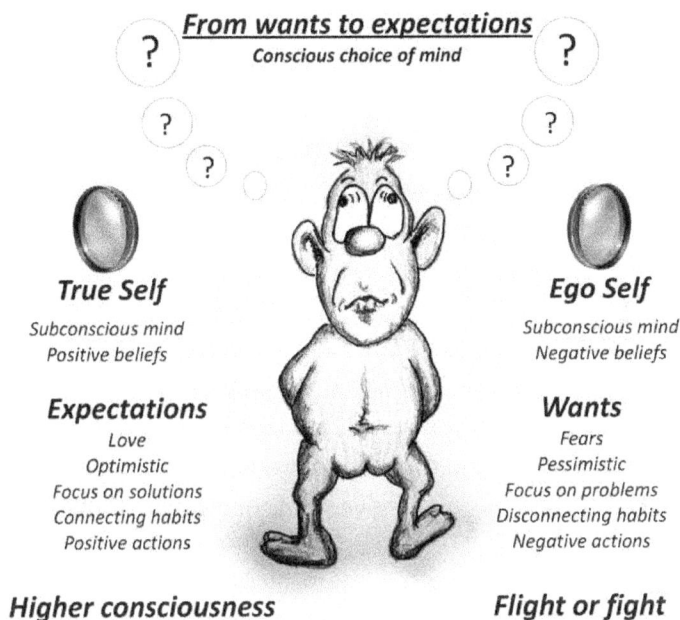

When we focus on wants our physiology changes to one of fear. And we have developed a terrific defence mechanism to deal with fear - our flight or fight response. This defence mechanism was fantastic to protect us from wild animals, but not so good when the threat is an irrational emotional fear. The release of adrenaline, noradrenaline and cortisol create uncomfortable feelings in the body. These sensations are designed through evolution to be uncomfortable. This discomfort creates a craving for relief from the threat. In the past we ran away and hid in caves, felt safe and went back to our normal state. Or we picked up a spear, killed or fought off the threat, felt safe and went back to our normal state. This defence mechanism has served us well over time and is one of the reasons we are on top of the food chain. It doesn't serve us well when it comes to irrational emotional fears created through the ego - the fear of lacking something. These emotional fears release the same uncomfortable hormones as they did in response to a physical threat - just as a meerkat stands on its back legs, head darting this way and that looking for physical threats. Our minds also dart this way and that, looking for and finding emotional threats that are not rational or logical.

The ego is just a programmed version of looking at the world in a threatening way through a filter of negative beliefs.

Negative focus

Now we might be starting to understand this defence mechanism, this ego, and we might be beginning to understand it isn't us. It's just a programmed version of looking at the world in a threatening way through a filter of negative beliefs. Much of it is created through the use of disconnecting habits and the withdrawal of connecting habits. - habits that we then turn on ourselves and continue to feed by our own negative self-talk.

We can now see that when we focus on the want for approval, control and security, we are expressing what we fear - we are lacking something. The mind now sees the future in a fearful way and we begin to feel anxious. Or we might go back to the past with regret, disappointment and guilt and feel down and depressed. We often skip between the two - between anxiety and depression. How could we possibly be happy with this frame of mind? By recognising it is only a frame of mind, a perception, *not reality* - just our perception of reality - just an illusion we create.

Negative focus
Conscious choice of mind

?

?

?

Choice

Ego Self

Subconscious mind
Negative beliefs

Wants

Focus is on problems
filtered through
negative beliefs

Negative thoughts
create
Negative destructive actions

Fear response

What I am holding in my mind I am bringing into my world by the way I think and act.

I recently gave a workshop for a bipolar support group. Now imagine two people at the back talking as I am giving my presentation. Let's also imagine I had an argument with my wife before going there. I would already be feeling disconnected and disempowered. My ego sees this situation as a threat. Listening is a connecting habit and my audience are not listening. The ego tells me they are probably saying that this is boring, rubbish and wondering what time will they get out of there. They don't approve of me. I want to control this. If they were children I would use disconnecting habits – for example: 'Stop talking now and listen, or it will be detention after class' - telling and threatening to control them. Now I have control I can continue. This is the fight response. The disconnecting habits are always the fight response. These are adults though. Threaten them with detention and they will laugh at me and walk out. All that's left is the flight response. I lose eye contact and my voice drops to a monotone as I look to get out of there as quickly as possible and go home to where I feel safe. Before long, everyone appears bored and looking at their watches wondering what time they will get out of there. What I am holding in my mind I am bringing into my world by the way I think and act. I begin to create the very thing I am afraid of. You see, the subconscious is a perfect servant. What you are holding in your mind it will bring into your world. It doesn't discriminate. That might give you some food for thought!

Positive focus

Now let's face it, I just didn't like the way the last scenario played out, so what could I do that was different? Well let's get back to the imagination again. I was filling in the gaps of what I thought was happening in a fearful way - with wants, wanting approval and control.

 **The subconscious can't tell the difference between a real or imagined experience.**

What I now choose to expect is that they are learning something and enjoying the presentation. I now think one was saying to the other. 'I use those disconnecting habits on my wife and she uses them on me. If we stopped using them we would get along much better and I probably wouldn't feel so depressed all the time.' Now I think they are listening and learning something. I release serotonin and dopamine - those feel good chemicals. I feel connected and empowered. I'm having fun and telling jokes and no-one is looking at their watch now. What I hold in my mind I will bring into my world.

The truth might be that one person was asking the other for a pen, but the subconscious can't tell the difference between a real or imagined experience. If I imagine they are saying bad things about me I will act in a way that brings this about. If I imagine they are saying good things about me, I will act in a way that brings this about. And in reality, they weren't talking about me at all. Interesting isn't it?

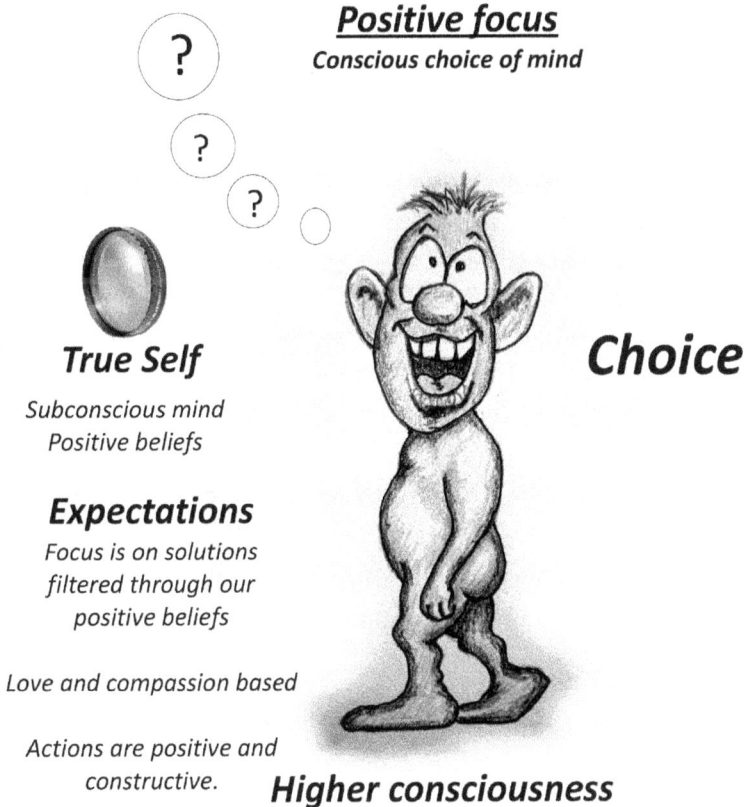

?

?

?

Positive focus

Conscious choice of mind

True Self

Subconscious mind
Positive beliefs

Expectations

Focus is on solutions filtered through our positive beliefs

Love and compassion based

Actions are positive and constructive.

Choice

Higher consciousness

Physiology of stress

Acknowledging how our minds affect the way we feel is to realise how our thinking creates changes in our physiology. We can also start to see what the Buddha was talking about 2500 years ago when he said that all of life is suffering and all suffering comes from craving. The craving comes from the intense desire for relief from the uncomfortable chemicals we release in the body when seeing the world in a fearful way

- from an ego point of view. Aggression, anxiety and depression are mind-created stressful states that strip us of our happiness. Let's face it; we are not going to be releasing serotonin and dopamine, (the feel good chemicals), if there is a sabre tooth tiger coming at us. We would be patting it on the head instead of running away! The flight or fight response works perfectly for real physical threats but is not so good for imagined emotional threats.

 ***Suppressed emotional issues will find their way out one way or another.***

If we look at our immune system we see it is designed to fight threats at a cellular level. Autoimmune diseases arise from an overactive immune response of the body against substances and tissues normally present in the body. In other words, the immune system mistakes some part of the body as a pathogen (a threat) and attacks its own cells. We know that continued stress will affect out health in a negative way. Could the cause of this be the body turning back on its self because we feel powerless to resolve an emotional issue or trauma – the suppression of this resulting in the body attacking itself? *Suppressed emotional issues will find their way out one way or another.*

Physiology of Stress

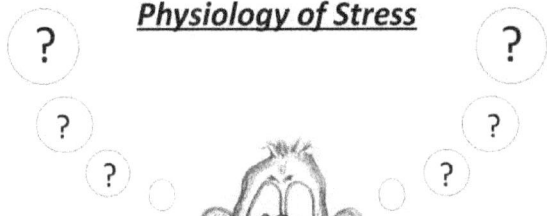

True Self

Optimistic

*Focus on cooperation
and contribution.
Happy and relaxed.
Increase in serotonin
and dopamine.*

Our natural state

Natural state

Ego Self

Fearful

*A stressful state
leads to an increase in
adrenaline cortisol and noradrenaline
in response to the fear.*

*Hyper arousal.
Anxiety
Depression
Aggression*

Flight or fight

Nothing is permanent and all things must pass.

Someone came up with this serenity prayer. *Grant me the serenity to accept the things I cannot change; courage to change the things I can and wisdom to know the difference.* Serenity is probably what the Buddha had in mind when he said to look at thoughts and feelings with equanimity as they continually rise and pass away. Nothing is permanent and all things must pass. Why get attached to something that is not permanent? But we do. We cling to the good feelings and have an aversion to the bad feelings. As we cling to the good feelings they soon disappear and our aversion to the bad feelings only perpetuates them but none of them is permanent. When we look at thoughts and feelings with equanimity, we are withdrawing the judgement of good or bad. This in turn stops the mind from seeing the threat and that in turn changes the body's chemistry.

Are you feeding the good wolf or the bad wolf?

Here is a story I heard or read a number of years ago. I believe it puts the ego and true self in a nutshell. It is about a wise old American Indian chief giving advice to his grandson. The chief says to his grandson.

'Grandson, there are two wolves inside us all, a good wolf, and a bad wolf, and they are fighting all the time. The good wolf is love, compassion, courage, generosity, fortitude, discipline, laughter and every worthy virtue a human being is capable of. The bad wolf is anger, hatred, laziness, jealousy, envy, greed, sloth and other vices a human being is capable of.'

The grandson looked at the old chief and said. 'But grandfather, if they are fighting, which one wins?'

'The one you feed is the one that wins,' said the wise old chief.

Which one are you feeding?

Our life experiences can cause us to doubt our ideals and our basic moral beliefs when we feel like a victim. It's not hard to see how some experiences might feed the "bad wolf". For many of us it might seem easier to feed the bad wolf, giving in to negative wants and giving up on virtue. To do so is to become a victim of yourself. To lose your moral compass is to lose yourself to fear.

What do you need to do now that you know this? You can choose the way you think and what you focus on. You can shift from wants to expectations. Let your feelings be your guide. If you are feeling down, upset, angry or frustrated; change your mind. If you don't mind it won't matter.

CHAPTER FIVE

The Mind is a Time Machine

There is no time but NOW!

If we were in possession of a time machine, we wouldn't go back to the worst past we could think of or forward to the most frightening future, but isn't that just what we continually do with the mind? We think back to the past with regret, disappointment and guilt. Then we think of the future with a want for approval, control or security – all the time seeing life in a fearful way. Looking at the past this way makes us depressed and looking at the future this way makes us anxious. We are not living in the present. And yet the present is the only time we really have. All else is just an imagination or a memory and can we really trust our memories?

I called into the town of my birth while on a business trip to Europe and was reminiscing with an old friend, Ron. I recalled an old memory from our childhood and remembered when this happened and that happened and who was there. Ron looked at me and said they happened at three different times and his recollection of who was there also differed to mine. I went over it again but our memories differed over the events of the past. Ron suggested we ask another friend, Michael, for his version to clear it up. Michael's version was closer to Ron's than mine. It was three separate events but his version was also slightly different. Three people with different memories of the same events left me feeling a little disturbed. My memory seemed worse than theirs. I always thought I had a good memory but that was now brought into question. I couldn't trust my own memory. I concluded on the long flight back to Australia that I would reminisce about these events half a world away. I would pull up these memories and pack them away again to a point where they eventually blurred into the same memory. Later I looked into false memory syndrome that had recently been pushed into the headlines. Children had been asked if they had been sexually abused and had it described to them until they developed a false memory of being abused. The imagination became a false memory. Although most abuse is real and not imagined, there are cases where the memory has been false. I began to realise that the subconscious can't tell the difference between a real or imagined experience. Portions of my own past have been coloured by my imagination and can't be trusted.

Depression often has its roots in the distorted past.

What is the point of continually going over negative memories with regret, disappointment and guilt when our version of the event might be an amplified distortion far worse than the event itself? If it was bad enough the first time, why continue to relive it over and over again in this time machine of the mind? The past can only serve to offer lessons and should be left behind so we can live in the 'now'. Depression often has its roots in the distorted past. There are some people in the world with full recall of all the days in their lives from around ten to fourteen years of age, but these are rare exceptions. The rest of us might have perfect memories locked away in our subconscious but the recall can be tainted, coloured, or even imagined.

Our imagination is our creative faculty. It's a tool, but do we usually use it as a tool? We can use this tool to imagine what we would like to bring into our life and then come back to this moment and do the things we need to do now to bring it to fruition. If you look around at all the man-made things in your surroundings, you will see how someone's imagination was at work as a creative faculty. All the things you see were at one time only in someone's imagination. We often use this imagination to worry about the future, thinking of the worst things that could happen. We kick in the want for approval, control and security and see the world as a fearful place, and most of the things people worry about never happen. What a waste of this wonderful creative ability!

What to do with this information? Understand your thought system is not you. It is a tool that we use to create. Learn to harness its potential to create a happier life and not let it run around like a bull in a china shop. Thoughts just bubble up in the mind but you don't have to listen to them. Turn your wants into expectations and dismiss or ignore the negative thoughts.

Anxiety has its roots in the imagined future - stuck in the wants for approval, control and security. Depression will often have its roots in the past with regret disappointment and guilt.

CHAPTER SIX

Our Judgements become Filters

Our judgements become filters of perception.

When we make a judgement we are saying this is good for me or bad for me - we are polarising our opinion. One example of this could be the weather. On a cold, wet and windy day someone might say they hate this type of weather. It's just weather, not good or bad, it just is. The judgement is a want for something different, but you can't control the weather. How many people give away their happiness by wanting to control something like the weather - something that is beyond their control? The judgement that this is bad for us creates the want. We might have a preference for something different but a judgement that cold, wet rainy days are bad will create a lot of unhappy days in our lives. Nature has a way of bringing these days into our lives when we want them least - as often happens when I plan to play golf!

Many judgements are made to the effect that something is good or bad - black or white. We no longer see all shades of grey. We create a filter of perception and the mind starts looking for everything that agrees with the filter and disregards the rest. We can see that filter at work for some people with regard to the weather. And isn't it interesting that we often call it bad weather?

If we withhold judgement we open up our perception to see all shades of grey. We are more likely to see reality than our limited, filtered view of it. Many judgements become beliefs and what we believe we will see.

The more judgemental we are the more we close down other possibilities.

A friend came to see me after losing his job. His boss didn't like him and had been looking for some excuse to get rid of him, and had finally found one. My friend said that this was the worst thing that had happened to him. I said it could be the best. He looked at me and said, 'I have just been sacked; how will that look on my future job applications? There is nothing good about this!' That was his judgement about his predicament. A month later he called to tell me he had a new job with more money and a great workplace environment and fantastic people to work with. Getting sacked *was* the best thing that happened to him. He had been putting up with a job he didn't enjoy, with a boss who had continually used disconnecting habits on him. His want for security had kept him there and the wants for approval, control and security were the cause of the judgement he made.

Our judgements create filters of perception just as our beliefs create filters of perception. The more judgemental we are the more we close down other possibilities.

I made some great big judgements about being short when I was a teenager. I wanted to be six foot tall (183cm) but I was only five foot five and a quarter inches (165.7cm) - and wasn't that quarter inch (6mm) important? If anyone asked my height, I would tag that quarter inch (6mm) onto the end because it made me more than five foot five. When platform soles shoes became fashionable in my teenage years I was overjoyed, I gained 3 inches (75mm) in a day! My joy soon diminished as every other teenager grew a similar three inches. I did however tower over my parents for the first time and that gave me some satisfaction.

I remember standing at a bar in a nightclub and turning around to see Phil Lynott from the band *Thin Lizzy* standing beside me. He must have stood over six feet six inches (198cm) tall with his six inch (15cm) platform soles. He stood there with this massive afro hair style and with legs as thin as my arms. I stood in awe. Tall and thin was in and Twiggy was the name of the super model favoured at the time because she was so thin. I just wasn't cool! I realised that genetically I could not compete with this level of coolness. I was in fact not born to be that cool.

I suppose we can be glad people like Van Morrison and Roy Orbison didn't make such judgements about themselves. Great talents would have been lost. We can see how judgements and beliefs can turn a good looking and very talented young man like Michael Jackson into something quite bizarre looking. All this was due to his judgements about his skin colour and looks.

I look at the tightened faces of some of the celebrities, resembling more a sculptured cat from a Pharaoh's tomb than the person they once were. And I see the artificial smile to hide the empty cat like eyes. They look like caricatures of their former selves. I see the conditioned ego afraid to grow old. This is the want for approval, control and security in action. You can't control your body as it ages. You can have an influence by keeping the body healthy but you have no real control. Botox and plastic surgery are just for cosmetic enhancement. This type of beauty is only skin deep although it might temporarily improve self-esteem for some if their self-esteem is so bad. True beauty really shines through from within.

There are also the judgments that plague many men about the size of their manhood. (My wife tells me I *am* a big enough dick without further enhancement!). Is the ego ever satisfied with what we have? More is more and less is less. Was I average, less than average, more than average? More would be good, less would be bad and the ruler won't lie. If you are waiting for an answer to that one you won't get it - I still have an ego! The last people I heard of who didn't have an ego were Christ and Buddha. It doesn't mean we can't be happy even with an ego. I don't bother about that question now. What is just is, and that's okay with me.

Withdraw judgement to see possibilities.

A client came to see me for anger management and a drinking problem. He came on a Tuesday and we discussed the want for control as the anger issue. The following Tuesday he came back and I asked him how he had gone. He wasn't drinking and was using the technique that I had taught him to release negative emotions. He had been feeling calmer and less agitated until Friday when he got his bank statement. When he saw that there wasn't much in the bank account he said he got angry, went out and bought a stack of beer, got drunk on Friday and Saturday but on Sunday was too hung over to get out of bed. He said he hadn't had a drink since, was back to using the releasing technique and was back on track. I asked him if there had been any more money in the bank on Thursday and he said no. 'But you were happy on Thursday so what changed on Friday?' I asked.

'I got the bank statement,' he said.

That was just a piece of paper with numbers; it didn't change anything. What changed was his judgement about his financial situation. When it wasn't in his awareness he had no judgement about it. It didn't affect him. When he judged it as bad, it created a want. He could just as easily have looked at it and thought about all the money he was saving by not drinking. That would have turned the want into an expectation. When it was not in his awareness it didn't exist for him. We will discuss more about this later.

It's interesting to note that while thinking about his lack of money, he wasted more on beer. What he was holding in his mind he was bringing into his world.

What can you do about this? You can withdraw the judgement of the situation or the person. Accept and allow the situation as neither good nor bad, it just is. You might have a preference for something else, but accept it and allow it to be just as it is, letting go of wanting to change it. Then look to see what possibilities can come from this. An example might be the judgement about the end of a bad relationship. You might look at the possibility of now finding a good relationship. We will look at a technique to let go in a later chapter.

CHAPTER SEVEN

The Essence of what we are

Try to find yourself. Am I this hand that I see before me typing on the keys? It looks like my hand; it has my wedding ring on it and my short stubby fingers. But am I these hands? Can I feel the wetness of the blood running through the fingers or the individual bones and muscles? No. Can I feel the finger nails or know the length of the fingers without looking at them? No. Can I feel where the skin stops and the air begins? No. I can feel some sort of vibration, but without looking at that hand I may as well have a hoof on the end of it. So where am I?

What about the heart? I can have a heart transplant and still be here. What about the brain? It can be damaged and I am still here. Some people have had half their brain removed and they are still here. It must be the feelings then. But most are just electro-chemical reactions caused by thoughts. I must be getting closer. The thoughts - but I was here before I learned a language which is the basis of this thought system - so I can't be thoughts. So I can't be found in the body, the feelings, thoughts - so where am I, because I know I am here?

The way to find out what is behind thoughts is to stop them. How do you stop them? Try watching for the next thought to pop up. What is the next thought that will pop up? - observe.

Did you notice the thoughts stop as you became the observer of them? So what is this observer?

 *The observer must be pure consciousness, pure awareness.*

So the essence of what I am must be this formless consciousness. You can slice and dice the body into the smallest parts and you won't find it because it is beyond form. It is formless which is why it is so hard to find. It can only be experienced - like love. It's like emptiness or a 'nothingness', filled with whatever we are aware of.

There are two things that can't be stressed. You can't stress nothing, because there is nothing to stress, and you can't stress everything. By definition, if it contains everything, there is nothing left to stress it. So the essence of what we are is stress free - until we break things down into individual things and judge these things as good for us or bad for us - creating a filter of perception. What's coming in through the senses is just information light waves, sound waves etc. It's just information in our awareness until we colour it through the filter of the belief/judgement system to give it meaning.

Now this is where things get interesting. If it is not in our awareness, it doesn't exist for us at that point in time. Let's take this a step further. I go to sleep at night and my awareness of this physical universe closes down; it no longer exists. I am blissfully unaware of anything going on around me. I wake in the morning and my senses again become aware of the physical universe. So here is the crunch. If this physical universe only exists for me when I am aware of it, I must be the centre of my own universe. The physical universe only exists for me, through my conscious awareness of it. If I am the centre of my own universe I must be the creator of it, and in co-creation with all the other billions of universes on this planet earth. If I am not here consciously, this physical universe can no longer exist for me. If one million people died in an earthquake on the other side of the planet, I would not be affected by it until I saw the news or read a paper. It would not be a part of my reality, not in my awareness.

The universe will continue to unfold through its own grand design and through the law of cause and effect, everything arising and passing away, evolving. But we still have a creative impact in our own little universe as we arise and pass away because we are also a part of this elegant design and are creative in our own right. We humans are evolving. Charles Darwin said that it was not the strongest or most intelligent of the species that evolves the best, but the most adaptable. We have used our intelligence to adapt to even the most inhospitable environments. In this way we are creative.

So what are you creating? Is it drama? What you believe is what you will see. If you wake up in the morning and see a world of drama, that's just what you will create through a filter system of beliefs and judgements. What is wrong with seeing the world and life as an adventure, a comedy, a loving place to be? This difference in perception is a world of difference in emotional experience.

Take a look at your life as though it is a movie.

Take a look at your life as though it is a movie - a movie with you as the main actor, director and producer. What type of movie would you like to create? A magnificent love story? Then see it as a love story and go out and create it. Like any movie it will have its twists and turns, its ups and downs; but life is a roller coaster. Are you too afraid to get on the roller coaster - sitting with envy while watching others having so much fun? On the first incline of the roller coaster we tend to feel apprehension. Wouldn't it be better to be back safe on the ground? Why did I do this? My apprehension might be building. This tends to turn to exhilaration once over the first incline when I realise there was nothing to fear but the fear itself. I see the people getting off the roller coaster with faces full of excitement, vibrant and full of energy.

I also see the people with fear in their eyes, too afraid to get onto the roller coaster ride. I like to see life as an adventure and a comedy. I laugh at the golf ball that heads off into the trees never to be found, (and believe me, this happens often in my game). I hit a little ball around a field. What's the point in getting upset at something that isn't really important in the scheme of things? We have even come up with our own rules. The thirty second rule can be used if you miss hit a ball off the tee and you can retrieve it in thirty seconds: No penalty. To see grown men charging after a miss-hit ball is hilarious. The *Gilly* rule was named after me: once you get to eight shots on a hole you stop counting. This rule was brought into play because of my request for a calculator at the end of most holes. You can invoke the Schultz rule, named after the TV program *Hogan's Heroes* for three shots during a game. When this rule is invoked everyone else has to say 'I see nothing' as you take the shot again. The leather wedge (shoe) can be used when you find yourself behind a tree. We play for fun, not competition.

A professional golfer asked me to caddy for him during a Pro Am. He was experiencing difficulty with anger and frustration - the want for control. On the first hole he stuffed up a shot and went one over par. By the fifth hole he was four over par and was getting more frustrated with every hole. I told him on the fifth that he had carried that first bad shot on his back for the last four holes. I asked him when he was going to put it down and let it go. I said he was four over, wasn't going to win, so he might as well just enjoy the day out. 'This is your psychological advice?' he asked.

'Yes, just let it go and enjoy the game.' I told him. He went three under par for the remainder of the game. On the way home I told him about our rules and he shook his head and said.

'You just don't care do you?'

I said, 'No, I am carefree but that doesn't mean I care less. I just don't take most things too seriously.'

Sometimes we need to just take off our heads and live through our hearts.

Judgements and beliefs stop us seeing reality and enjoying the moment. To enjoy the moment and experience the essence of what we are we need to get out of our heads and away from the *paralysis of over analysis*. Accept what is, clear the mind of judgements - and you will find peace.

What can you do to create a happier life? You can first accept that you are the creator of it. See your life the way you would like it to be and then live it that way. What you are holding in your mind you will bring into your world. This is the power of choice.

CHAPTER EIGHT

We all Live in an Illusion

Imagine sitting still in a valley on the stump of a chopped down tree, with the roots still deep in the earth creating a solid foundation. It is just before dawn. The night is quiet and you are waiting for the sun to rise in the sky. Across the valley is the silhouette of a mountain in front of a night sky covered in bright twinkling stars.

The first hint of red appears behind a mountain and the lower stars begin to fade as the sun begins to rise. An orange glow forms behind the mountain and the birds come alive with their dawn chorus. There is glow of light over the mountain as the sun begins to rise, turning the sky from black to blue. The stars begin to fade from view and the shadow of the mountain retreats across the valley like a swarm of ants running from the light. The sun continues to rise until it is high above the valley and the valley is full of life.

Now let us take a look at reality.

Nothing in the universe is still.

Go back until just before dawn. Place your imagination into the tree stump - into the roots gripping the soil and boulders below. Then place your imagination into the Earth itself - this magnificent Earth hurtling through space on its orbit around the sun. It is travelling at over 100,000 kilometres per hour. Imagine you can feel the large mass of the Earth hurtling through space with incredible accuracy. It rotates on its axis and you are sitting on its surface travelling at 1670 kilometres per hour if you are on the equator. As you look across the sky, you see the mountain moving across the starry night sky, as the large mass of the Earth rotates on its axis with such power and precision while hurtling through space. It's rotating to a point where the sun's rays hit the atmosphere above, turning the sky red then orange and obscuring the stars from view. There is a glow of light as the mountain begins to move across the face of the sun while the Earth rotates on its axis. Small particles in the atmosphere scatter the light and turn the sky blue - the stars fade from view. Birds wake and the shadows recede across the valley as the Earth continues to revolve on its axis. The mind is under the illusion that we are sitting still and the sun is rising. Nothing is still. Even the atoms in a stone are travelling faster than we can comprehend.

Imagine now looking at the Earth from a place out in space - the blue greens of the sea and the greens, browns and yellows of the land. Swirling white clouds and snow covered polar caps and mountains rotate slowly on the Earth's axis while it all hurtles through space. Imagine the dark side with tiny lights around the coastlines highlighting the darkness of the sea and sparkling like a diamond necklace in the night.

Imagine the Earth half bathed in darkness and half bathed in light. See this Earth revolving out of darkness and into light, and out of light into darkness. Can you see time? Can you see yesterday or tomorrow? Even time is just an illusion created in the mind. Zoom in until you are over a city watching people like ants rushing back and forth so earnestly, taking everything so seriously. How small are our lives in the scheme of things? How insignificant. Everything in this magnificent universe arises and passes away as it continues to evolve. Nothing permanent and nothing still. This universe is evolving through the universal laws of cause and effect; of chaos and stability; and in patterns that no longer seem random. Such an elegant design - evolution based on universal laws that don't discriminate. The butterfly effect from the chaos theory suggests that a butterfly flapping its wings in Australia will eventually have an effect on weather patterns in New York. In turn, each choice you make will lead to a different future - even the smallest choice. Billions of people make billions of choices creating a myriad of possible futures - all interconnected. Each choice is a cause that will have an effect on the future.

A quark is an elementary particle and a fundamental constituent of matter. Quarks combine to form composite particles called hadrons, the most stable of which are protons and neutrons - the components of atomic nuclei. This computer I type on has more space between the atoms than the atoms themselves. The more we look at matter, the more we see the illusion of it. There is more space than particles, and every particle broken down is more space and less matter. Yet I type on this computer under the illusion that it a solid matter. It is just energy vibrating at different frequencies creating the illusion of something solid. We think we can comprehend this world through our limited senses but we have no idea. My dog runs to the door when my son's car enters the bottom of the street. He must hear and know the sound of the car. I can't hear it or recognise it, but I know he is coming. My dog tells me so. If I go to meditate in my bedroom, that same dog will seek me out and sit by my side throughout the meditation. I have no idea how he knows or why he comes at this time – but he is there without fail; and if I lock the door he will scratch to get in. There are many things we can't comprehend, yet still we know through experience. There are many things we can comprehend and yet still live with an illusion of something different because of our habits of thinking - our conditioning.

Everything is borrowed then left behind.

Most choices we make come from the illusion that we require approval, control or security to be happy. It's an impossible illusion to satisfy - nice to have but impossible to get. Another Illusion is that we own anything. Everything is borrowed and left behind. My car, my house, my wife, my children and my money are not mine – none is permanent. All one day will be left behind. All that we really leave behind is our influence on others. A kind word and a smile is your legacy. This will remain long after your house has fallen to bits and your car has rusted itself out of existence.

The ego thinks in terms of the little me, the little mine, the little I. The ego is under the illusion that it is you, and we are often under the illusion that *it is* us. It is the ego that hides reality behind an illusion of often irrational and illogical limiting beliefs. Then life becomes all about me, what's mine and I need more. Where can I find me in this body with thoughts and feelings that are impermanent, continually arising and passing away? There is no permanent me! What could ever possibly be really mine when I enter this world with nothing and leave with the same? Who am I? A psychotherapist, father, grandfather or husband - I can find myself in any of these situations - they are just roles I play. The ego latches itself onto this - I, me and mine - like a parasite latching onto a host.

There are things we can't perceive through our limited senses, but we know them to be true because we experience them. I can switch on a light and see the effect of electricity but I can't see the electricity. My mobile phone rings and I am soon speaking to a friend who could be on the other side of the world. I can't see the radio waves or even know how they can get through the walls and windows. I just know that they exist because I experience them. Science looks to find ways to harness the elegant design of this universe of energy for our benefit. We may not understand or need to understand the science, but we can see the truth of it in our experience.

Our emotional experience of life is often something we don't understand. We tend to look outside for its cause. This is the illusion created by the ego. All we emotionally experience is mind created. Everything outside is just information coming in through the senses. It's how we chose to perceive this information that creates the emotional feelings. The cause is our perception and the effect is our feelings. This is the point where the great illusion begins and is the domain of the ego.

The ego likes to blame everything and everyone outside of us for our suffering. The Dalai Lama came to Australia a few years ago. The Prime Minister and the leader of the opposition had still not agreed to meet with him because of pressure from the Chinese government. When asked what he thought about this he said, 'I will be happy if they would like to meet with me and I will be happy if they don't.' The Dalai Lama was not about to let his happiness be affected by something he had no influence over. There was no want for control or approval - no illusion - just an acceptance of what was true. He didn't take it personally. There was no effect on his feelings.

What can you do with this information? You can see the wants for what they are, an illusionary fear. And what is this fear? I came across this definition from a book by Giovanni Lordi, *Toolbox 4 life,* **F**alse **E**vidence **A**ppearing **R**eal. Maybe we can define a want as **W**aiting **A**nxiously, **N**ever **T**rue.

CHAPTER NINE

The Root of all Craving

All craving comes from wants.

I was once told that 50,000 thoughts are bubbling up in a person's mind each day and many of these thoughts are the same thoughts. I don't know how anyone managed to count them but the figure is irrelevant. We have thoughts bubbling up into our consciousness on a continuing basis. The thoughts are meaningless until we make a judgement about them and create a want. Wet, cold weather is the example we turn to again. Weather is not good or bad unless the mind perceives it as so. We have positive and negative thoughts arising and passing away. When we attach ourselves to a thought, we perpetuate it and strengthen it by thinking about it. We give it energy, we are feeding that thought.

The ego wants us to be a victim.

Positive and negative thoughts bubble up. They have no real impact upon the way we feel until we start thinking about them. If we make a negative judgement we create a want for something different - we fear we are lacking something. This fear releases adrenaline, noradrenaline and cortisol as a fear response to a threat thus creating uncomfortable feelings. These feelings perpetuate more thoughts as the mind continues to resolve a threat which in turn perpetuates more feelings. The cycle of the thought/feeling system creates a craving for relief. This cycle can turn anxiety into panic attacks or frustration into anger. It can overwhelm us. Now we can understand the Buddha's statement that all of life is suffering and all suffering comes from craving. Stuck in our heads we go off to the future with a want for control, approval and security - thus creating anxiety. Or off we go to the past with regret, disappointment and guilt - creating depression. We are not living in the moment and the ego tells us we have every right to feel depressed. This is the stubbornness of the ego and the resistance to letting go. The ego wants us to be a victim - only as a victim can it survive. Its role is to protect us from being a victim, so we need to be a victim to require its protection. It was created from a victim mentality and much of it was formed prior to the development of a rational logical mind. The mind of a child is like a sponge. It is vulnerable to soaking up negative comments and taking them personally. What might seem a fair punishment for an adult, will often be seen as a personal attack by a child who has yet to develop a fully rational and logical mind.

It is the reaction, with a liking or disliking, craving or an aversion, that creates our suffering - our craving for more or less.

The sense organs are lifeless unless consciousness comes into contact with them. The function of consciousness is just to know without differentiating. Then the next part of the mind starts working - perception. Our judgement of good or bad is based on memories of past experience. Next, the third part of the mind starts working with the creation of sensations. The judgement that it is good for us will create pleasant sensations and the judgement that it is bad for us will create unpleasant sensations. These sensations arise in the body and are felt by the mind. The fourth part of the mind now begins to work - reaction. Someone says something nice to us and the pleasant sensations arise. We like them and crave more. Someone says something nasty to us and we create unpleasant sensations and we start disliking them. We have an aversion to them and crave freedom from them. It is the reaction, with a liking or disliking, craving or an aversion, that creates our suffering - our craving for more or less.

Let's take the example of a smoker to understand craving. Smokers start to smoke usually at an early age because they want to feel connected to other smokers. They want to feel empowered, important, grown up and cool. Most don't enjoy that first cigarette - not at all - but they persist until years later, all that is left is the habit of wanting a cigarette twenty or thirty times a day. The mind thinks of the cigarette and perceives a lack. Sensations arise in the body from the judgement that a cigarette would be good for me and the lack of a cigarette would be bad for me and the reaction is a craving for it. Once we get what we want the craving subsides. Now the smoker is off to the airport to go to Singapore. First the bags are checked in then it's quickly outside for a smoke. This cigarette isn't doing much to satisfy the cravings because the mind is thinking about the next nine hours without a cigarette. The want to control the next nine hours is beyond the smoker's control. The smoker is chain smoking outside the airport - the craving unsatisfied.

But sooner or later the smoker must board the plane. Do the thoughts stop? No. One hour into the flight and the mind pops up the thought, 'I could really do with a cigarette.' It's a pointless thought because you can't get what you want so the thought is dismissed, ignored, forgotten about and the craving disappears. This isn't the end of it though. There are triggers. The smoker likes a cigarette after a meal and this triggers the want for one. This again is dismissed. It's pointless wanting something you can't have. The craving is less on the plane than it was while chain smoking outside the airport. If it isn't in your awareness you won't crave it. The craving subsides until the smoker gets close to their destination where the possibility of getting a cigarette gets greater. The longest part of the trip for a smoker is often at the baggage carousel waiting for the bags to come out at the end of their journey. Once outside the airport smokers can return to their twenty a day habit of wanting – creating a want then satisfying it. Now we can see at the point of perception we can dismiss, ignore and forget the wanting and with it the reaction - the craving.

It is amazing how many smokers, through just the understanding that they are not slaves to nicotine but slaves to their own habitual wants, can dismiss, ignore and forget the thoughts as they arise. In doing so, they relieve themselves of the cravings. I also tell smokers to plant a positive expectation by telling themselves they don't want cigarettes and don't need them. They are healthy non-smokers.

What about thinking through the heart? Now you might question how you can think through the heart. It is less about thinking and more an instinctive feeling that can precede the thoughts and balance the mind to postpone reacting negatively. This is also not about the physical heart but the essence of being in the moment, this moment *now*, with allowance and acceptance and a positive expectation. Expectations are positive, flexible and focus on a solution. Wants are negative, rigid and focus on a problem. Looking at people through the heart, the feelings precede the thoughts if we are in the habit of feeling love and compassion for others. This can be more an instinctive process developed through understanding. Through the head the thoughts precede the feelings: Now a little story to get a greater understanding of how it works.

My office is across the road from a major hospital. We have a lot of people who illegally park in our private car park to save the seven dollar hospital parking fee. One day I arrived to find our car park full but for one parking place. Only the surgery next door was open and I was sure the surgeon didn't have nine clients at the same time. I concluded that many of the people parking there were from the hospital across the road.

I opened the office and headed to the front to get the mail just as a man was parking his car in the last parking space. As he headed towards the hospital I mentioned that this was private parking and I had clients coming with nowhere to park. He said he was just popping across to the hospital to pick something up then coming back for an appointment with the doctor in that office, pointing to my office. I told him that I worked there, was not a doctor and he didn't have an appointment with me. He pointed to a second office and said it was that doctor there. I told him the person in that office was also not a doctor but an orthotics specialist and was closed for holidays. His rage erupted and I was getting called all the names under the sun before he threatened to knock my head off my shoulders. He then marched off to the hospital shouting, 'Get the car towed you idiot, think I care.'

In previous years my ego would have bought into that. I would have met harsh words with harsh words, threats with threats. I would have taken it personally. The ego takes things personally but these days I tend to take a different approach. The disconnecting habits used by this man are the result of his feeling disconnected and disempowered in his own life. This is his problem, not mine - unless I take it personally. The ego wants to buy into this and take it personally. Have I a right to be angry? He has abused me, threatened me and lied to me. I have every right to be upset but I would rather be happy. It's a seven dollar car park for Christ's sake. What's the point of losing your happiness over a seven dollar car park?

There are many things a man can take to appease his tortured pallet, but it won't appease his tortured soul.

I did feel a surge of adrenaline but it was soon let go through a technique we will cover in the next chapter. My first thought was '*interesting*'. Interesting is one of the best thoughts we can get into the habit of using - It make us the observer instead of the victim. A shift to the heart is next. I don't know why this man is behaving this way but I know he is suffering. Maybe he is an angry man all the time - continually frustrated with how life has treated him. Maybe his wife is in the hospital dying of cancer or his son has been in a car crash and he has been looking for a car park for the past twenty minutes. I don't need to know the reason for his suffering to feel compassion for him; and compassion is a form of love that comes from the heart. From the heart I feel before I think and therefore the thoughts are of love and compassion. From the heart I felt compassion – from the ego I would have felt hurt and angry. It is after all not my problem and so I leave it behind. As I looked out the window while opening the mail I saw him return to move his car. He wouldn't even have made it to the hospital before the thoughts of his car getting towed away and the cost of getting it returned entered his head. By the time my first client arrived there were three spare parking spaces available. I could have got into a fight over a seven dollar car park for nothing. Did I give my power away? Many would suggest I did. But by not reacting I held onto it. We give our power away when we buy into the problems of others and take things personally. How could it be personal - he would have behaved like this with anyone who questioned him.

So how do we break this cycle of reaction? The next chapter will answer that.

CHAPTER TEN

How to Release Negative Emotions

If you are not releasing negative emotions - you are suppressing them.

The thought/feeling system is a circular system that feeds itself. The thoughts feed the feelings and in turn the feelings feed the thoughts. Or looked at another way, the thoughts create the sensations we feel and the sensations we feel perpetuate the thoughts. The sensations create a craving for relief and the mind looks for relief through the flight or fight response. Frustration can develop into anger and anxiety that can develop into panic attacks through this feedback system. Just like the feedback of an amplifier that continually gets louder and louder deafening the ears or, in this case, overwhelming the mind. We can create an uncomfortable rage or an overwhelming fear through this feedback system. We must realise that the brilliance of the subconscious mind is its ability to learn through the development of habits. But the subconscious mind is not discerning about the habits we create. It can create good habits as well as bad. It is our reaction to the sensations that must be the point at which we begin to work. The judgement or perception of something as being good or bad for us creates the want and with the want comes the craving for relief.

We might now look now at the Buddha's Awareness Meditation - becoming aware of the sensations arising and passing away in the body and looking at these sensations with equanimity. They are not good or bad - just sensations that arise and pass away. Some are unpleasant sensations and some are pleasant - but none is permanent. If they are not permanent they are not me, not I, not mine. We cling to the pleasant sensations and have an aversion to the unpleasant sensations - a craving for more or a craving for less. Now I am not so sure about you, but I have a family to support. I can't head off into a cave to practise meditating on this for the next seven years - but I can learn a lot from this that allows me to be much happier now. The Awareness Meditation is about acceptance and allowance to break the cycle of reaction and craving. If we look at the root cause of our negative emotions coming from the want for approval, control and security, then we can use this as a starting point to learn to release and let go of these negative emotions.

Many of our problems come from the suppression of these negative emotions. It's like adding skins to an onion; the onion grows. The universal law of cause and effect would indicate that if we plant bitter seeds, at some time in the future we will have to harvest a bitter crop. The wants are the bitter seeds that grow to create a bitter harvest in our lives. Learning to release and let go of the negative emotions is like peeling back the skins of the onion. At its centre we begin to realise that there is nothing to fear but the fear itself.

So how do we release and let go of these wants? We must release our attachment to them before we can let them go. What are we attached to? We are attached to being the victim: attached to our judgements, that become filters. It is the ego's attachment born from being a victim and perpetuated through victim mentality. So we become a victim of our ego-self, and the ego is like a scavenger dog. It is always scavenging for something or someone else to blame for the way we feel. The ego is a protection mechanism which requires us to be a victim for its survival. But it's the ego, not us - just a conditioned response.

 *It is okay to have thoughts and feelings. This isn't good or bad - it just is!*

We must bring a problem into our awareness if it isn't already there. We will make a judgement about this as being bad for us and creating a want for something different - a craving for relief. The first step is to allow those thoughts and feelings to be there by telling yourself, 'It is okay to have these thoughts and feelings. This isn't good or bad - it just is.' Telling yourself you don't want to change them. Here we are trying to withdraw judgement and accept what is. We might have a preference for something else, but at this point we are looking at an acceptance and allowance of what is in this moment: the withdrawal of the judgement about it. You might at this point want to look at the problem. The threat: is it a want of approval, control or security? It might be all three, such as in the case of jealousy. You don't really need to know what want it is to get an acceptance and allowance of it, and to tell yourself, 'it is okay to feel this way.' Through allowing and accepting the thoughts and feelings we are telling the mind that this is not a threat. If your mind stops seeing it as a threat, you stop releasing the adrenaline, noradrenaline and cortisol that create those uncomfortable sensations. We break the thinking/feeling feedback cycle of reaction. Now we need to relax into these feelings with an allowance and acceptance. It is okay to relax into an allowance and acceptance of these thoughts and feelings and just let them be. As in meditation, we are moving to a point of looking at the thoughts and feelings with equanimity, without judgement - not good or bad for us - they just are. Where in meditations we are looking at all sensations, with this method we are working on specific problems creating the thoughts and sensations and our judgements about them. You can of course use it just to focus on the feelings. Can I find myself in any of these thoughts and feelings? You will find you can't find yourself in any of these thoughts and feelings. Can I just let them go or do I want to remain a victim of them? Why would you want to remain a victim of your own thoughts and feelings? Can I accept them as they are without judgement and then let them go? Yes. Will I accept them as they are and then let them go? Yes. When? Give yourself permission, say '*Now*'. Then just withdraw the judgement about them and relax into an acceptance and allowance of them. I often find it beneficial to say now with a sigh as I breathe out and relax into them. In this process we are giving the mind permission to let go of the attachment to wanting. For some, the feelings can be like a stress ball in the stomach area. I used to imagine the ball dissolve as I let go. It could be butterflies that disperse, or just breathing out a black cloud of negativity. Use your imagination to find the way that works best for you. You want to be able to disperse or dissolve the feelings in some way. This technique is not much different to what the Buddha taught in awareness meditation, looking at the feelings with equanimity. Not good or bad. Giving permission to accept and allow them to be, and not seeing them as a threat. The process is similar to a part of the 'Sedona Method' developed by Lester Levenson, and taught by Hale Dwoskin. The Sedona method takes you through a number of processes to release emotions. I found the program to be very practical, beneficial and recommend it. Like any process, it can be adapted to suit yourself.

The process to release

Get in touch with the thoughts and feelings of something that bothers you and say to yourself.

Accept that it is okay to have these thoughts and feelings. This isn't good or bad. It just is.

It is okay to feel this way.

It is okay to relax into an allowance and acceptance of these thoughts and feelings without judgement, and just let them be, just as they are.

Can I find myself in any of these thoughts and feelings?

Can I just let them go, or do I want to remain a victim of them?

Can I accept them for what they are, without judgement and then let them go? Yes.

Will I accept them for what they are and then let them go? Yes.

When? Now…………..

This process might sound simplistic but often the simple things are most effective. Practised often enough the process becomes a habit. All that I have left of the process is an internal sigh as I breathe out. I no longer need to go through the full process and I often find I have released the emotion automatically without doing anything. I supply a CD to my clients that they listen to each day to establish the technique and develop the habit of letting things go. I find the CDs are effective therapy - a cheap and effective way to have a therapy session each day without my even being there. An MP3 of the technique can be downloaded from my website at: www.melbournehypnosis.net.au.

We often find ourselves swimming against the current of life.

Many people worry about things they have no control over. Does this serve any purpose? No. The vast majority of the things we worry about never eventuate, but we get stuck with an attachment to the problem. We get stuck wanting something different - feeling we are lacking something that stops us being happy. Look back at all the things you worried about a month ago and you will see what I mean. It was a waste of time and energy. You always get by - you always get through. Stuck in negative thinking it is often hard to see a solution. Sometimes there is no solution other than to let go and just go with the flow. We often find ourselves swimming against the current of life, feeling as though we are drowning in it. Even if we are successful swimming against the current, we will only find smaller rivers and streams. Eventually we end up on the rocks. When we learn to go with the flow, we drift into an ocean of good feelings. Learning to release negative emotions is learning to go with the ebb and flow of life. Let's now look at some examples of this technique.

I was up early one morning working on the end of year financials to send to the accountant while my wife, Julie, went grocery shopping. After finishing the financials I allocated time to upload Dragon voice recognition software on my laptop. I had hoped that I might get away from this two finger typing and be able to dictate much of this book to save time. I soon found my version of the software was not compatible with Windows 7. I searched the net and found version 10.1 was compatible but the reviews of its compatibility left a lot to be desired. While looking through the reviews I found that Windows 7 has its own voice recognition software. I spent the next half hour training the software to understand my voice. I entered this document and the first sentence translated perfectly. The second sentence had something about Lebanon in it and wasn't anything like what I wanted to say. After a few more sentences and with a sigh, letting go, I returned to my two finger typing. Soon I noticed the clock ticking away. In thirty minutes I had to be at the office. I still needed to do a water change on the fish tank and that would take all of the thirty minutes. My wife arrived back from her grocery shopping and dropped two very heavy bags on the floor before going out to the car for more. On her return she looked at me filling the fish tank with buckets of water and said, 'I need to get myself a new husband.' She wanted my help but I didn't have time. Of course the ego wanted to respond to this. I had been busy all day and was rushing to leave for work on time. The ego wanted to take it personally. Instead I thought, 'interesting.' *Interesting* is one of the best words we can use to stop taking things personally. It makes us the observer rather than the victim. Something else I often say is this: 'Is what I am about to say going to bring us closer together or move us further apart?' If it will move us further apart I bite my tongue and keep quiet. In short, I accepted and allowed the thoughts and feelings to be there and then let them go. On the way to work I reflected on my wife's words. I recalled that when she awoke that morning she had mentioned she had hardly slept due to a pain in her side, and thought she might have a kidney infection. She wouldn't normally say something like that, so I put it down to her not feeling well. She was fine when I returned home that night.

CHAPTER ELEVEN

Our Suffering creates our Motivation to Change

One choice can change our future.

The Buddha in his first *noble truth* said that all of life is suffering. We don't like to suffer but we do suffer. Let's take a look at 'Chaos Theory' to understand the need to suffer.

Chaos Theory studies the behaviour of dynamic or open systems that are highly sensitive to initial conditions. A *dynamic or open system* is a system which continuously interacts with, and is influenced by, its environment. Human beings are a dynamic or open system that can be vastly influenced by small changes in conditions. This chaos theory effect is popularly referred to as the *butterfly* effect. The name of the effect was coined by Edward Lorenz, a meteorologist. It is derived from the example that states that a small thing, such as a butterfly flapping its wings, can create a ripple effect that could have an influence in the creation of a hurricane several weeks later. It was discovered that even the smallest changes will have an impact on future weather conditions. There are a number of movies that use this theory to base different outcomes on different choices – leading to many different conclusions. I like this theory. It suits my stronger needs for freedom and fun. *One choice can change our future.* Our future is created by the choices we make now. We are the creators of our future – creators in our own right.

The Chaos Theory suggests that an open system will continually change and develop to a point of turbulence before transforming into something stable. Out of chaos comes order.

We can see this in evolution. It is the organisms that adapt best to changing environmental instability that survive. The instability creates suffering and the suffering creates a requirement to adapt and change - to evolve. If you don't adapt and evolve you don't survive. Just ask the dinosaurs. We don't really know why they became extinct but we can be fairly sure it was because they couldn't adapt to changing conditions. (The only thing I know about dinosaurs is that they had big feet, were supposed to generally have had small brains, and that I wouldn't have wanted to be following one around the back garden with a pooper scooper!)

It is suggested by science that the earth is 4.5 billion years old. 2.5 million years ago the Genus Homo appeared. 200,000 years ago man started looking much like he does today and 25,000 years ago Neanderthal man became extinct. Physically, we have not evolved much in 200,000 years. However, we have evolved consciously over a relatively brief period. Julian Jayne suggests in his book, *The Origin of Consciousness in the Breakdown of the Bicameral Mind*, that human consciousness as we know it is fairly new and was a leap in our evolution over a short period of time. Jayne suggests that human consciousness did not begin far back in animal evolution. It is a learned process brought into being out of an earlier hallucinatory mentality by cataclysm and catastrophe only 3000 years ago and is still developing. It's interesting to note that many religions use the same time frame for God breathing life into the creation of man.

 With this leap we became self-conscious and this was probably the beginning of the development of the ego. Because of this leap in consciousness, I now sit typing on this computer and receive emails from half way around the world in the blink of an eye. I turn on a tap and water pours out, flick a switch and the room lights up. Humans are masters at adapting - but still we suffer. We know the body won't evolve during the course of our lifetime (although mine seems to be evolving into a wrinkled, slightly balding, saggy version of what it once was), but the mind can evolve and adapt. Maybe those enlightened souls of the past were examples of the next step in the evolutionary ladder. Christ said, 'You too can do these things.' The Buddha called it the eradication of suffering, which must be the pinnacle of evolution. I find this an interesting concept. All that is, God if you like, becoming aware of itself through human consciousness. Yet, it is just a concept. I am not enlightened enough to know if it's true or not. We can take this concept to its extreme. Suppose we all become enlightened, and eradicate all our cravings; would we still want sex? Let's face it, you don't hear much about those enlightened beings from the past having kids after becoming enlightened. Without babies the human race would cease to exist. We would become extinct. Interesting thought: extinct if we don't adapt and possibly extinct if we reach the pinnacle of adaptation. Probably not - there can be great joy and love in sexual union; it can be much deeper than satisfying the basic sexual urge we are genetically disposed to for procreation.

We see so much anxiety and depression in the world today but often don't see this as an opportunity to evolve.

So a leap in consciousness may have been brought about through suffering and our ability to adapt. Suffering in this context would indicate that it creates the motivation to change, to evolve. We see so much anxiety and depression in the world today but often don't see this as an opportunity to evolve. A pill is prescribed and popped like a band aid, covering the root cause of the problem which, in most cases is our thinking. No one teaches us how to think - how to use this amazing computer as a tool for positive creation. And it is a tool. We didn't have this thinking system until we learned a language. And the development of metaphor to expand language created a different thinking system. It is not us. It is a learned tool.

Stuck in our thoughts, and looking at the world in a fearful way, we create our own suffering.

But we have become addicted to popping pills to make us feel better and relieve the suffering we feel. Irving Kirsch is a professor of psychology and specialist on the placebo effect. He is also author of the book, *The Emperor's New Drugs*. Drug companies claim that the effectiveness of antidepressants has been proven in published clinical trials showing the drugs worked significantly better than placebos. He suggests that a closer look at the data shows that the difference between the drug response and the placebo response is not clinically significant and that many of the effects of antidepressants seem to be due to the placebo effect. What is the placebo? A placebo is nothing more than a sugar pill that works on the belief system. If you believe you will feel better - you will. Back to what we believe we will see. This belief system is so powerful.

So, our suffering can be the catalyst that brings about our transformation like a caterpillar turning into a butterfly. From chaos comes order. I don't know about you but I don't like the idea of changing brain chemistry with a pill. There will obviously be cases when this is required due to a deficiency in the system - the body not working the way it should. If the mind isn't working the way it should then, in most cases (though not all), if we change the mind we resolve the problem. But we have become a society looking for a quick fix and instant gratification.

A young man came to see me. He had been diagnosed by a doctor with social anxiety disorder, and was prescribed medication. He wanted my advice before he bought the medication. In his hand he held a booklet describing the symptoms he was experiencing. This booklet had been printed by the drug company supplying the medication he was supposed to take to fix his problem. Nice little box with high walls to put someone in. I knew him and his problem and it wasn't social anxiety.

This young man's girlfriend had ended their relationship two months earlier, and he had taken it personally. He felt he wasn't approved of. He also wanted the security of the relationship, as he still felt an attachment to her.

It wasn't personal. She had thought she was too young to be in a full-time relationship.

He had stopped seeing his friends and didn't have much money because he was going to college three days a week. He hadn't had a part time job for eight months and so couldn't afford to run his car, or go out with his friends. He was isolating himself. He wasn't getting out of bed until lunch time most days because he was feeling so disconnected and disempowered and was slipping into depression. Prior to his girlfriend ending the relationship he was one of the most sociable young men you could meet. Within a few weeks of understanding that he was creating the way he was feeling, and could choose to create something different, he had a part time job in a surf shop. This worked around his studies and also enabled him to take a job delivering pizzas at night and that covered his car costs. He also found some work at the weekends in a hardware store. This put money in the bank. He was mixing with his friends again and he soon found himself with a new girlfriend. *He did it all without popping a pill.*

I have many clients coming to see me who are already on antidepressants. I don't advise them to stop. I don't believe in kicking away the crutch before they can walk. Antidepressants change brain chemistry and stopping them dead can create problems. I suggest they work to get their thinking right first and then work with their doctor to gradually reduce the dose over time to come off the medication.

If we look at our suffering as the chaos required, that creates the motivation to change and adapt, then we can see it for the gem that it is. Out of the muddied pond the lotus flower rises and blossoms.

What can you do with this information? Embrace your suffering and see it as an opportunity and motivation for change - an opportunity to evolve.

CHAPTER TWELVE

Ego States, Anchors and Triggers

Evoke the power of positive states – you've got them!

We have looked at the ego as the accumulation of negative limiting beliefs. Let's look at this in a bit more detail. Let's say that each negative belief is a mini trauma from the past that was formed during a state of fear. The fear may have formed a feeling of helplessness or a feeling of not being worthy, of not being approved of. It could, for example, also be just insecurity that formed through loss or a feeling of not being safe or just being scared. It could have come from a time when we were bullied by someone, or maybe, as a young child, when we had just lost our parents in a supermarket. Or possibly a time when we felt abandoned, rejected or unable to live up to our parents' expectations. The possibilities are endless. The resultant beliefs are based on a fear of lack, a lack of approval, of control, of security.

At the time of this trauma, a state of fear would have presented itself, resulting in the flight or fight response - a basic physiological survival mechanism in response to a threat; a threat that could be physical or emotional in form. A belief is formed to protect us from future threats. In the event of a future threat, the belief will form a state of fear - an ego state similar to the initial event; a feeling of not being safe; or of being unworthy, just to name a few. These beliefs are limiting us from reaching our full potential, they keep us stuck.

We don't only have negative beliefs, we also have positive beliefs. These beliefs are usually built from an accumulation of positive things that happen to us: having loving supporting and encouraging parents; standing up for ourselves against a bully, or protecting a friend or younger sibling and being treated with respect. It could come from our achievements at school or in sport, or from overcoming a perceived problem. The beliefs formed create feelings of confidence, empowerment, worthiness, approval and security. These beliefs don't limit us; they grow as we build on them. They create positive states. When we feel threatened, the negatively threatened ego state will rise to the executive position and take control to protect us. It will take charge to become the dominant state. When this happens we sometimes no longer have access to the more positive states.

The negative ego states are anchored to an event. Similar events or situations will trigger an emotional fear response and this may result in a phobia of sorts. The things that can trigger this response are many and varied - often just imagined. A fear of public speaking has its roots in the past, as do phobias about snakes, flying or lifts, etc. The triggered ego state creates the anxiety - the fear of the future that dominates the imagination with this perceived threat. Logically the mind knows that there isn't anything to fear, but the subconscious is not rational or logical. The ego state refuses to listen to the logical mind; it takes control. In this state, other more positive states are ignored and protection is paramount. The traumatized ego state is running the show.

The ego states are a function of the thought/feeling system but many negative ego states can be established from a response to a traumatic physical threat. For example, my own feeling of claustrophobia was experienced when trying to snorkel for the first time. My inability to take a breath with my head under water may well have come from breathing in water at bath time as a baby. This was overcome through desensitization by repeated practice with a snorkel - just as the phobia of speaking in public can be overcome through desensitisation by practice.

I had a client who told me she would spontaneously vomit at the smell of a certain aftershave. She was gang raped at the age of fourteen and one of the rapists was wearing this aftershave when it happened. It was a subconscious reaction. I am continually amazed at how much pain we humans can inflict on each other - especially emotional pain that can last a lifetime unless resolved. And most of the time, the perpetrator is probably unaware of the extent of the damage they actually create by their actions. It, in most cases, must be a result of the damage done to them at some time in the past.

Traumatic ego states often require therapy, to gain access to more positive states and allow the traumatized ego state to feel safe enough to allow positive states to play their part. Often we can gain access to the positive states through the use of anchors and triggers. It makes sense that if we can anchor and trigger negative ego states, then we can anchor and trigger positive states. The interesting thing is that athletes have been doing this for years, many without even knowing. The footballer who continues to wear the lucky underpants he was wearing when they won the championship two years earlier is doing so to trigger the anchor from that day. The routine of pulling up of both socks and then throwing a piece of grass in the air to test the wind before taking the kick is another example of triggering a state of mind - a positive state. Often in our work our negative ego states limit our ability to achieve all that we can. A fear of public speaking or cold calling clients is a good example. A negative ego state created through being rejected, not feeling approved of, or not feeling worthy, can create a barrier to achieving our full potential. Procrastination can be a result of this. We know what we need to do, but are afraid to do it. What if we get rejected? What if we are not approved of? What if we fail? We end up treading water and going nowhere, doing nothing. We need to step out of our comfort zone, and sometimes we need access to a positive state to do this. This is where anchors and triggers come in - to change our state.

A sales company sent one of their sales representatives to me for sales development. During one session we identified four potential new customers who could increase his sales and margins by 20 plus percent. He was given the task of setting up appointments with them. He returned two weeks later and made every excuse as to why he hadn't had the time to make contact. The negative ego state, fearing rejection, which is the want for approval, had created the procrastination. I had him imagine a time when he felt really confident, not concerned with failure or rejection. He thought about his time as a junior footy coach, a time when his football team was playing in a final. They hadn't expected to get that far, and he told the team it wasn't about winning but about playing the game to the best of their abilities. Regardless of the result he would be proud of them for trying. They won the game. I had him imagine giving this pep talk to his team and getting all the feelings associated with this event. I then had him clap his hands and rub the palms of his hands vigorously together so he could feel the heat from the friction between the palms, while saying in his mind, 'okay, let's just do it.' I told him to practise this over the next week. And anytime he felt he was putting things off, to clap his hands and rub the palms together while saying in his mind, 'okay, let's just do it.'

The purpose of this action is to anchor a positive resource - a positive state to a past positive experience. We can then trigger, through this anchor, the state of the positive experience when needed, to overcome the negative ego state. By the following appointment with me he had made contact and had appointments with the new potential customers. He had also found them quite accommodating and realised there had been nothing to fear but the fear itself.

 *The way we feel is usually a result of the dominant state at the time.*

This simple anchor and trigger technique can be very powerful. I use it in my work with athletes to get them focused or fired up, or for public speaking to create a strong expectation of a positive result. It can also be used for phobias, such as flying, to motivate and push past the fear, or overcome situational anxiety such as pre-exam nerves, or social anxiety. It is designed to trigger a positive expectation and overcome procrastination from a base of positive states. Change your state and you change your mind and the way you feel. The way we feel is always a result of the dominant state at the time.

Anchors and triggers can be many and varied, and sometimes we don't realise we are triggering negative ego states. Our state is often reflected in our posture. A person feeling depressed will sit with head bowed and shoulders slumped. Just changing the posture by pulling shoulders back, head up or putting a smile on the face can change that state and the way we feel. Most followers of sport have seen the posture of a team that has already given in to defeat - they have dropped their heads, we might say. What they have actually done is to change their state to one resigned to defeat and failure, and this is reflected in their posture. It's hard to feel bad when you are smiling

Let's cover the technique to anchor and trigger a positive state. First, we must access a positive experience from the past where we felt confident and motivated, or we can create this from an imagined future experience. For example, in public speaking we can imagine giving the presentation, being dynamic and giving it with confidence and passion. We are creating all the feelings we would feel hearing the applause and kind words afterwards.

Once the state of confidence, calmness, excitement, achievement, etc. is achieved, it needs to be anchored. I believe the best anchor comprises of two elements, an action and a feeling; such as clapping the hands together and rubbing the palms to generate heat. I have also used rubbing the thumb and forefinger together. It can also be as simple as straightening the strings on a tennis racket between shots, or bouncing a basketball three times and saying 'focus' each time to create a focused concentration. Imagine or remember a positive experience, and get in touch with the positive feelings you would feel from this happening; then anchor. The more it is practised the stronger the anchor to the feeling and positive state. We are anchoring the good feelings.

I can't help but be excited and motivated to action by just rubbing my hands together. This trigger gets me excited. I use it prior to giving workshops and seminars. It is also useful when I need to get motivated to do an account reconciliation or quarterly tax statement - not amongst my favorite chores!

Our vocabulary also triggers ego states.

I have long since dropped the words 'angry' and 'frustrated' from my vocabulary and replaced them with 'perturbed' and 'interesting'. I have no ego state that can latch onto the word 'perturbed'. In fact the word makes me laugh to myself. I have never developed an ego state association with the word *perturbed* the way I have developed an association with the word *angry*. If I say to myself that I am angry, an angry ego state pops up. If I say I am frustrated, a frustrated ego state pops up. If I say that's interesting, I become the observer of the situation and not a frustrated participant. Hate is another triggered ego state that is often used with such abandon - from food to traffic jams or people or professions or even work. 'I hate being stuck in traffic', you might say, without realising how it will make you feel. It can't help but make you feel bad, and yet it isn't good or bad; it just is. Why feel bad about something you have no control over? The negative words you use to describe your situation will trigger a negative ego state and the associated feelings.

I often tell a client who presents with depression to remove the word 'depression' from their vocabulary. It represents a long dark tunnel with no end in sight. I tell them to say they are down, and they can pick themselves up; or sad, and they can do something to make themselves happy. With anxiety I will tell them to say they are just scared, and ask themselves 'what am I scared of?' A lot of the time they are just scared of being anxious! A fear of fear.

Our negative words are often anchors from the past that will trigger the negative ego state. Remove the negative words from your thoughts and conversation and you can't help but feel better. Use positive self-talk especially when talking about yourself, or your life situation to yourself or to others and improve the way you feel. If you are using disconnecting habits on yourself with your-self talk, you reinforce the ego and the negative state.

Let your posture reflect the way you want to feel - confident, relaxed, alert and happy. If you are happy, you will infect others with your happiness. Let your words be positive, not negative, and learn to trigger positive states then notice the difference in the way you feel.

CHAPTER THIRTEEN

Comfort Zones

Your comfort zone is either expanding or contracting.

Comfort zones, what are they?

We are always in a state of expansion or contraction, growing or shrinking, progressing or regressing. Let's take our muscles, or even better, the muscles of a football player, or athlete, for example. After a period of rest and reduced activity, at the end of a season, the muscles have begun to lose strength and shrink before the training for the new season begins.

Those first few training sessions result in stiffness and soreness as the muscles get pushed beyond what has become comfortable use in the off season. They start to feel discomfort. The athlete must push beyond what feels comfortable to grow in strength, fitness and endurance and this will continue throughout the season. Every time they push past what is comfortable and break through that comfort zone they are growing. If they don't push past that comfort zone they are stagnating or regressing.

This push past the comfort zone must be done gradually to avoid injury. This is true for athletes and also true for our emotional comfort zone that is the limit of the positive beliefs we have about ourselves - the limit of our positive self-esteem.

To grow we must do things that make us feel uncomfortable.

Outside our comfort zone are the negative limiting beliefs about ourselves; the ego. The ego is always telling us we are not good enough, not accepted, not approved of and not worthy. Many of these beliefs were formed when we were children - when people used disconnecting habits on us, or withdrew connecting habits - beliefs formed before we had a rational faculty of mind. Imagine a ball full of positive energy, positive beliefs, sitting in the centre of a field of negative energy and negative beliefs. The field of negative beliefs places pressure and stress on the ball of positive beliefs and the positive beliefs are pushing back - the ball expanding and contracting. For the ball to expand, we must push past negative beliefs that make us feel uncomfortable. To grow we must do things that make us feel uncomfortable. The negative beliefs form a barrier we must push through.

Let's take a look at public speaking, said to be the number one fear of many people. Why is it a fear? It's the want for approval. The fear that people won't accept the way we look, what we have to say or how we are saying it. If we take a logical look at this fear, we can see it is an irrational fear and without justification; impossible to satisfy. It is impossible to get the approval of everyone. In fact it is almost impossible to get one person's approval all the time. If I could get my wife's approval all the time it would be fantastic, but in reality it won't happen, I am not perfect. If you had 51% of people's approval, you could become prime minister of the country. This limiting fear, the fear that we will not be approved of, is the discomfort we feel pushing back on our comfort zone, making us feel uncomfortable. Our comfort zone is the limit of our positive beliefs.

The amazing thing about expanding your comfort zone is that, when you tackle one limiting belief, many other similar ones fall away; you grow exponentially and increase your self-esteem. When we are growing, our self-esteem is high and when we are shrinking, our self-esteem is low. When it comes to public speaking, every time you push past the fear it becomes easier. But, like anything, it must be done gradually. In my experience, it can take 4 to 6 weeks to change the habit patterns of the mind.

I had a friend who had no problem with public speaking. He said he loved it and asked me what the difference was between him and so many others that seemed so terrified. I told him that he expected everyone would like him and didn't bother about wanting their approval. He agreed that he did expect everyone to like him. I looked at him and said: 'Not everyone is going to like you.'

'That's their problem not mine' was his reply.

Apart from comfort zones formed by the way we have been treated in life; we can also develop a fear from a trauma that can become a phobia, or a problem with anxiety or depression. If our comfort zone is limited by a phobia, sometimes the cause of this phobia isn't self-apparent. Let me tell you about a phobia I discovered in myself in my late twenties.

The first time I went snorkelling was in my twenties. Friends gave me a mask and snorkel and we waded off into the sea. I was looking forward to seeing this new underwater world. I put my face into the water and could not for the life of me take a breath through the snorkel. I was crippled by fear - something was telling me I couldn't breathe with my face underwater. Lifting my head from the water and looking around at my friends all snorkelling away, I tried again but the breath wouldn't come. My ego being what it was at that time, I watched my friends snorkel and as each one popped his head up I held my breath, put my head down and pretended to snorkel. When we returned to the beach I told them how much I'd enjoyed it and was off to buy a mask and snorkel for myself. Over the next month I would get into the bath each night and practise. One or two breaths on the first session, but increasing as the days went on until I could spend a full hour with my head submerged, breathing through a snorkel. Not one to do things by halves, my next trip to the beach was to scuba dive. I persuaded a friend who scuba dived to take me out and teach me to dive. We jumped out of his boat with a compressor running in the background feeding air to the regulators in our mouths. Thirty feet below us was the sea bed. I was bobbing like a cork on the surface when he suggested that I might not have enough lead weight around my waist. I didn't like the idea of carrying this lead anchor around my waist, but I was told it was required to compensate for the buoyancy of the very uncomfortable and very thick wet suit he had arranged for me to wear. I told him I thought the current weight would be fine. Breathing out, he started to descend. Breathing out, I was still bobbing on the surface like a cork. Eventually he was on the bottom when I decided to duck dive down and, thrashing like a fish out of water I made it to the bottom. The first thing I noticed was the excruciating pain in my ears, and the second thing I noticed was my feet were still pointing to the surface. Upside down, I grappled with the weeds on the sea bed to try to keep myself on the bottom. He gave the thumbs up signal rehearsed in the boat. With both hands busy, I smiled and the water filled the mask. Like an unguided missile, I launched out of the water breeching like a hump - backed whale.

We returned to the boat and removed my mask to find it filled with watery blood. 'Didn't you equalise?' my friend asked.

'What's that?' I asked. The vacuum from the water pressure had sucked blood into my sinuses, I found out later.

 ***We extend our comfort zones by releasing the negative emotion attached to the fear.***

'Maybe we should give it a miss', he said. I knew, at that point, that giving it a miss would mean I would not be coming back. We adjusted the weight. I learned how to equalise the pressure and I dived for the next thirty minutes without pain or a problem. Within three years I was a scuba diving instructor. Within five years I was teaching instructors and diving in the limestone caves of South Australia, my comfort zone well and truly extended. This extension of my comfort zone had been through desensitisation. Each small step outside the comfort zone tackled the limiting belief and I was growing exponentially. Had I not tackled this limiting belief, I would have missed out on a whole range of wonderful experiences, and a whole group of new friends in the process. We extend our comfort zones by releasing the negative emotion attached to the fear.

We can overcome limiting beliefs and extend our comfort zones regardless of the cause of these limiting beliefs. By extending our comfort zones we increase our self-esteem and grow as people. The limiting beliefs are not you; they are irrational fears designed to protect you. But in the end they only limit you. They are just an electro chemical process in the body, created by an electro chemical process in the brain, created by negative conditioning from the past. They are a distorted view of who you are - an illusion of who you are.

The workplace is often a place where people work within their comfort zones unless a positive environment and culture is created to change this. If a boss manager uses disconnecting habits on employees, they will be afraid to fail, and this closes down creativity. They will be afraid they won't be approved of. The comfort zone of a person under a boss manager will contract and shrink as the disconnecting habits tap into limiting negative beliefs.

With a lead manager we will experience the opposite - the employee's comfort zones will expand and grow as the connecting habits are used on them. They will become more creative and push to achieve greater goals with positive expectations. They can step out of their comfort zones with support and encouragement. They will enjoy an environment and a culture of challenge, support and encouragement.

To grow as a person we need to take on challenges that make us feel uncomfortable. When we look at goal setting we will see that the goals should be big enough to scare us a little and excite us a lot.

When you start to step outside your comfort zone you begin to realise that there is nothing to fear but the fear itself. So go out now and do something that challenges you; do something that makes you feel uncomfortable. Push yourself beyond your comfort zone, increase your self-esteem and grow into your true self.

CHAPTER FOURTEEN

Goal Setting and Time Management

Everything we do comes from a goal set in the subconscious mind.

Walt Disney once said that all dreams come true if you have the courage to pursue them. I always introduce clients to goal setting; it creates a positive expectation of the future - something many people don't have. Goals motivate, excite and create momentum.

How many dreams have you squandered in your life through lack of action and commitment? We have all had dreams, but often we lose sight of them as the trivialities of day to day existence take us away from pursuing them. These are trivialities for which we often sacrifice our important dreams. These short-term wants takes us away from our long-term aspirations - away from our goals and our dreams. What we will be covering in this chapter are the simple steps of goal setting and time management.

I had a client who worked for IBM. I suggested we look at goal setting and, he told me he had recently done a five day course on goal setting so it was probably pointless. I asked what goals he had been working on since the course and he said he hadn't developed any yet. I think it might have been a case of too much information. You need to keep things simple for them to be effective and I would be at a loss to cover effective goal setting in more than one hour. I like to keep things simple.

Everything we do is goal orientated; it's the way the mind works and most goals are designed to meet our needs in some way. Just getting up to make a cup of coffee starts as a goal in the mind. With goal setting, we are looking at setting goals that help us grow. Because of this a goal should be big enough to scare us a little but also excite us a lot. Sometimes it is fear that stops us achieving our goals. Fear of failure can stop us dead in our tracks. Sometimes we just feel overwhelmed by the things we need to do to reach the goal, or the time it will take to reach it. Sometimes we feel that we just don't have enough time. Well you can't eat an elephant in a single sitting but you can eat it one bite at a time. Some simple steps can overcome these barriers.

Around 3% of people write down their goals - only 3%. But it has long been recognised that the 3% are the ones most likely to reach their goals.

Working on three to five goals on a continuing basis allows us to achieve the things we would like on a regular basis.

Let's first look at goals from a business point of view. How far do you think we would get if we said let's build a 20 storey building over there and not write anything down? How far would we get if we didn't turn it into a project and plan the activities from design to construction? It might seem ridiculous but that's exactly what most people do when it comes to their own goals. Your own goals and dreams need to be turned into personal projects - some large projects and some small projects. When you can see your goals as projects, you can plan the activities to accomplish them; you can move them from wishful thinking to reality. I believe that working on three to five goals on a continuing basis allows us to achieve the things we would like on a regular basis.

Let's again look at the project of building a 20 storey building. The goal first must start in the imagination of someone. If you look around and see all the man-made things your eyes come to rest upon, you can understand that they all started out in someone's imagination - chairs, computers, cars, cups, clothes and that's just to name a few! They all started out as someone's dream. All started out as an imagination that moved to a business project that materialised through planning and activity. In business we can be quite good at allocating time and resources to the bigger projects and yet still not see most of our work time as *working on a project* time. There should be times for maintenance that can also be a project. If we are not working on projects of growth, then there is a good chance we are stagnating or going backwards.

What is time? Can we actually make time, lose time or buy time? Not really. Time is just a period of measurement. As the earth rotates on its axis, it gives us periods of days, and as it orbits the sun gives us periods of years. All periods of time for humans are psychological time - we created them. We break the days into hours, and the hours into minutes - but it is all created in the minds of people. Some organisms have their own sense of time, such as the corals on the great-barrier reef. They spawn once a year over a two day period - but this is a result of environmental conditions. They don't follow the human clock. (And they chose to spawn a few days after I spent a week in Queensland waiting to see this marvellous thing happen!)

You can't manage time; but we can plan time to manage activities. It is a psychological resource - a resource given in the same amount to everyone every day. It's the activities you choose to perform and the management of these activities within a set time frame that determines whether goals are being achieved. So we can't make time, but we can take the time we have in this moment to do what's important. We can take the time to plan and perform activities each day that will move us closer towards our goals.

So, let's look at the mechanics of goal setting. I believe it was Napoleon Hill in his book *Think and grow rich*, who first said, 'what you can conceive and believe; you can achieve.'

So, the goal or dream starts in the imagination as a concept. We start to visualise the finished result. Because the subconscious mind can't tell the difference between a real or imagined experience, the more we hold the goal in our imagination, the more real it becomes for us. It becomes believable - and when it is believable the subconscious mind moves us towards it, what we believe we will see. Maxwell Maltz wrote a best-selling book called '*Psycho-Cybernetics*' back in the seventies - psycho being the mind and cybernetics being a guidance system much like we see in a plane or a guided missile. A plane or guided missile may be off target over 95% of the time but it keeps checking progress towards the target and altering direction to suit. When we imagine our goal as realised on an ongoing basis the subconscious mind works the same way. It becomes creative in checking progress and changing direction, if required, to get back on track.

 ***We need to turn the want into an expectation and know we will achieve it.***

To make sure we hold the goal in our imagination we need to write it down with a time frame and visualise it frequently. When writing down a goal, always write the goal with a time frame and as though it is already realised - this creates a positive expectation. We don't want to hold it in our mind as a want. This will just tap into the fear that we may not get what we want. We need to turn the want into an expectation and know we will achieve it. I have a ring binder exercise pad to write down my goals.

I worked with another Psychotherapist as his supervisor. When he first came I mentioned the benefit of giving clients CDs for use between sessions and suggested he would benefit from doing the same. Each month he would come along for supervision and I would ask how his CD was coming along, only to get the same answer: 'I've started the script but haven't had the time to work on it.'

The following is the way I turned the idea of the CDs into reality. This comes directly from my goal book and it is this simple.

The Goal.
By the end of November I have three new tracks to add to the car CDs.

To Do.
Track name

Ego states	~~Write script~~	Record
Attitude	~~Write script~~	Record
Moment	~~Write script~~	Record

A script for a 15 to 20 minute recording will take me around four hours to write. I will record the three tracks together and allow eight hours for recording, editing and adding music. Total time is twenty hours. I take the ego states script and book two 1 hour sessions in my diary each week for the next two weeks. I scribe a line through this to let me know it is in the diary. At the end of the two weeks this is now complete and is highlighted with a yellow highlighter. The next script is then allocated time in the diary and a line scribed through it. The above example tells me I have two scripts finished and one in progress and I am now looking at booking in the eight hours for recording.

The more yellow I see, the more motivated I become to achieve the end results. This goal was achieved over a seven week period. I write 'completed' through the goal when finished and leave a few of these completed goals in the front of my goal book. This tells me each time I open my goal book how good I am at achieving them - simple, but very effective.

It is the same principle for personal or business goals. Holding the goal in the imagination is the first step to achieving it. But our management activities make the difference between achieving a goal and letting it drop off the radar.

Now this is where we need to look at a goal in the same way as a business looks at a large project: with a list of things to do; plus a list of activities that needs to be completed for the goal to be realised. So we put together a 'to do' list with all the activities needed to achieve the goal. I always suggest that you have an exercise book where you write down your goals and list the activities to do.

This might be a 'to do' list for the person wanting to get fit and lose 5 kg.
- Forty-five minutes of exercise 5 times a week.
- Limiting eating treats to twice a week. Small treat.
- Eating healthy food for all meals. Higher protein lower carbs.
- Two meals open choice. No restrictions on type of food.
- Five alcohol free days a week.

Now we know what to do, we need to schedule when to do it in a diary. Schedule the exercise on five days at the times you plan to do it. Nominate two days when treats are allowed and two open choice meals. Decide when you will have the alcohol-free days and nominate them with an 'AFD' in the diary. As this is a repeating schedule it can be duplicated each week in the diary, and in this case the project would run until the end of the year. At that time, you might consider retaining some of the key elements, such as exercise, as a maintenance program. The main thing to recognise is that you must keep the appointments with yourself. You must do what you have recognised you need to do to reach your goal or you will be drifting around the ocean like a ship without a rudder. Once you have scheduled your actions and given them a time-frame during your day, your goal is already realised. You just need to keep these appointments with yourself. But you have to be careful. In will pop the short term wants, 'I can't be bothered exercising today, I just want to stay in bed an extra half hour.' To overcome these wants we need to maintain the desire and motivation to reach the goal. We need to create a belief in its success - a positive expectation of a successful outcome. We need to develop the habit of doing what we need to do.

Your subconscious mind can't tell the difference between a real or imagined experience.

In the case of this goal, each day you could visualise yourself as being fit and healthy and 5kg lighter, and feel the way you would feel if you were. Feel the way you would feel if it were already realised. It is our imagination, coupled with emotion, which creates the belief. Your subconscious mind can't tell the difference between a real or imagined experience. You might go through your goals each day and check progress towards them or you may find it suits you to do it once per week when you schedule the activities from your 'to do' list, but you should have your goals in your imagination at least once per day to maintain momentum and expected progress towards them.

There is another benefit from scheduling your day in a diary. It frees your mind to live in the moment - to be fully focused on the task at hand and this in turn makes you more efficient. Our minds no longer jump back and forth thinking I have to do this and that - it's all planned and in the diary or on the 'to do' list. And we can also have a daily 'to do' list for all those things that crop up from time to time that are not part of our goals.

Sometimes we can begin to feel overwhelmed by all the things we need to do. Listing and scheduling them takes our minds off them. We don't need to think about them until we do them. One of the most important things to schedule into your diary is a time each week to review your goals.

So let's review the basics of goal setting and time or activity management.

Firstly, see your goals as personal projects. Write them down with a time frame, and state them as though they are already realised. Have a goal book that you review at least once a week.

Secondly, break the goal down to activities you need to do to reach the goal. A 'to do' list.

Thirdly, schedule the activities into a diary and keep these appointments with yourself. Scribe a line through the activity in your goal book when you scheduled it in your diary. Highlight the activity in yellow in the goal book when it finished.

Do what you need to do. Keep these appointments with yourself and just do what you need to do in the moment.

Lastly, visualise them every day as you move towards them. As you do the activities and review them at least once a week, highlight the activities finished and schedule the next activity in your diary.

I see goals as organic and not set in stone. Sometimes goals will change or develop into something else. Let them grow and change if they need to. Below is a photo of my goal sheet with regard to writing this book and you can see in an instant my progress towards my end result; you might also notice the book you are reading had grown with more chapters and words.

1/6/11

By the end of the year I have written + published a book
"Psychology of Success".

25,000 words
Allow 250 word/hr
= 100 hrs
Finish writing by midOct.
10-11 week - 10 hrs per wk

1. Detail chapters
2. Write chapters
3. Load of voice recognition software
4. Send 1st few chapters to chair for feedback
5. Have edited
6. Send to publisher
7. Make change from feedback

1. Introduction
2. Mind
3. Habits + needs
4. Relationships
5. Time life
6. Essence
7. Judgement
8. RAS
9. Craving
10. thoughts
11. Comfort Zone
12. Goal Setting
13. Religion
14. Ego States

CHAPTER FIFTEEN

Purpose, Sociopaths, Integrity and Ethics

Understand yourself and understand others.

Purpose.

Philosophers have pondered over the meaning of life for thousands of years - the purpose of it all. Am I here to claim to know the meaning of life? Well, not exactly. It's more about the meaning of our needs - the purpose behind our needs. If our needs drive our behaviour, there must be an evolutionary purpose in the development of them. William Glasser, a psychiatrist and developer of reality therapy and choice theory, came up with the theory of these basic needs, and the habits of communication. When we look at them they make sense and are simple to understand. If we understand the purpose of our needs we can see the purpose behind the evolution of them.

Let's now look at these needs again - the needs for love and connection, empowerment, freedom, fun and survival. We can see that our needs are more complex than the needs of other animals. This could be the reason why we are at the top of the food chain. The complexity of our needs could have been the catalyst for our leap to a higher level of consciousness - a conscious choice as opposed to just basic animal instincts to survive. With conscious choice comes responsibility. Some don't like the sound of that, but *responsibility is just the ability to respond – the ability to make a choice.*

Survival is the basis of all needs - every living thing has this basic need. Many mammals developed the need for love and belonging. They suckled their young and many of them banded together in groups for protection. This gave mammals an increased level of survival. Then the need for power came in. We can see this in the animal world, with stags banging heads together, and silver-backed gorillas banging their chests (not much different to the way some people behave today). The strong and powerful also dominated the mating game and had a better chance of surviving and creating more offspring and strengthening the gene pool. Human beings then developed into a different species to anything else.

We could now choose how to think. Of course the strong were still dominating and so freedom entered as a need - the freedom from the power of others - to be free from their domination in order to survive. For the more advanced consciously, I suggest the need for power was being tempered by a need for empowerment. This is more about recognition and having an influence over one's life than power over others. A high need for power over others conflicts with the needs for love, connection and belonging. It frustrates this need. The need for fun - to experience new things, to learn new things - also developed from basic play. The more we learned; the more love, connection, empowerment and freedom we could get and the better were our chances of survival and the survival of the human race.

 Human beings began to spread across the world in conquest of others, or freedom from others. Some were still driven by the base need for power - others shifting to empowerment. These set up groups that were more co-operative and democratic. Let's face it - that's what being human is all about. These needs have developed to bring human beings together in co-operation and contribution for the benefit and continued propagation and survival of the species.

It's a bit like a cell in the body. The cell's co-operation and contribution to the whole perpetuates life in the body. If it takes more than it gives, it becomes cancerous and threatens the life of the body. The purpose of our needs is simple and based in the need for survival – co-operation and contribution to the whole. If we look at our purpose, it is co-operation and contribution first to family and friends, then to the broader community, and then to the whole of society. The purpose of business is to provide a positive service to society and in doing so, be paid for this service. The basic purpose of government is to make sure all people have food, shelter and freedom from harm - to provide systems of health care and education, and to protect the environment for future generations. The problems we see in society today all around the world come from the failure of governments, businesses and individuals to recognise our true purpose. It often takes something like a devastating tsunami to wake people up to the need to help those less fortunate - to begin to feel love and compassion for our fellow man - to change our focus from what I can get, to what I can give. The ego is all about getting.

We have a responsibility to meet our needs and, in doing so, we meet the needs of others. If we are living for a purpose of co-operation and contribution, we can't help but meet our needs. So what stops us living with this purpose and meeting our needs? Thinking we can't be happy because we lack something, and this creates a want for more - more money, more possessions, more approval, more control, more security.

What is integrity of a system? There is a box of tissues on my desk. The system has integrity if it holds the tissues in place and allows me access to the tissues, one at a time. It serves the purpose for which it was designed. What if the bottom dropped out of the box? The system would lack integrity. It would not serve the purpose for which it was designed. So integrity and purpose go hand in hand.

Sociopaths

There are many psychological disorders that we can come across in society, but there is one in particular that I would like to cover with regard to integrity. Why single out this one? Because we often think people with this disorder are normal and exhibit normal behaviour. I refer to the sociopath. Sociopaths can blend into society, and I have had to work with quite a few over the years. They often leave a trail of destruction behind them and much pain and suffering for others. They feel no remorse, guilt or empathy - they lack integrity. The sociopath has a purely egoist point of view – it is all about them. A sociopath will usually be a bully, but a bully might not be a sociopath. I focus on sociopaths because I see them as extreme form of ego – giving the appearance of control but they are usually out of control. Why? It's because of their high want for control.

Let's take a look at the profile of a sociopath so that we can recognise them when we come into contact with them:

- Glibness and superficial charm.
- Manipulative and conning.
  Sociopaths never recognize the rights of others and see their self-serving behaviours as permissible. They appear to be charming, yet are covertly hostile and domineering, seeing their victim as merely an instrument to be used. They may dominate and humiliate their victims.
- Grandiose sense of self.
  Feels entitled to certain things as *their right*.
- Pathological lying.
  Sociopaths have no problem lying coolly and easily and it is almost impossible for them to be truthful on a consistent basis. They can create, and get caught up in a complex belief about their own powers and abilities. Extremely convincing and even able to pass lie detector tests.
- Lack of remorse, shame or guilt.
  Sociopaths have a deep seated rage, which is split off and repressed. They do not see others around them as people, but only as targets and opportunities. Instead of friends, they have victims and accomplices who end up as victims. The end always justifies the means and they let nothing stand in their way.
- Shallow emotions.
  When sociopaths show what seems to be warmth, joy, love and compassion it is more feigned than genuine and serves an ulterior motive. They are outraged by insignificant matters, yet remain unmoved and cold by what would upset a normal person. Since they are not genuine, neither are their promises.
- Inability to love.
- Need for stimulation.
  Sociopaths are living on the edge. Verbal outbursts and physical punishments are normal.
- Callousness/lack of empathy.
  Unable to empathize with the pain of their victims, having only contempt for others' feelings of distress and readily taking advantage of them.

- Poor behavioural controls/impulsive nature.
  Rage and abuse, alternating with small expressions of love and approval produce an addictive cycle for abuser and abused, as well as creating hopelessness in the victim. Believe they are all-powerful, all-knowing, entitled to every wish, no sense of personal boundaries and no concern for their impact on others.
- Irresponsibility/unreliability.
  Not concerned about wrecking others' lives and dreams. Oblivious or indifferent to the devastation they cause. Do not accept blame themselves, but blame others - even for acts they themselves obviously committed.

Other Related Traits:

Contemptuous of those who seek to understand them. Do not perceive that anything is wrong with them. Authoritarian. Secretive. Paranoid. Only rarely in difficulty with the law, but seek out situations where their tyrannical behaviour will be tolerated, condoned, or admired. Conventional appearance. Goal of enslavement of their victims. Exercise despotic control over every aspect of a victim's life. Have an emotional need to justify their crimes and therefore need their victim's affirmation (respect, gratitude and love). Ultimate goal is the creation of a willing victim. Incapable of real human attachment to another. Unable to feel remorse or guilt. Extreme narcissism and grandiosity.

Have you seen these traits in people you have come in contact with? Many sociopaths reach high levels in business and politics. Sociopaths are not interested in co-operation and contribution. It is all about the base need for power and control. They have very little need for love and belonging. It is all about satisfying wants at any cost. The need for power has its roots in the want for control, approval and security. It is good to look at the sociopath. They are all around us creating great destruction. Hitler, Saddam Hussein and Gaddafi are examples. Many politicians are more subtle in their quest for power but still show sociopathic tendencies. Sociopaths seem to be stuck in an evolutionary time warp and lack integrity - the needs of a silver-backed gorilla with the intellect and ego of a human. The sociopath is the domain of the ultimate ego mind.

Integrity

 **The integrity of the system of contribution and co-operation repairs itself and evolves.**

The human condition has evolved through the development of our basic needs. These needs have evolved through co-operation and contribution. History has shown that a sociopath's behaviour and the resulting destruction they cause, usually leads to their own self-destruction. Out of chaos comes order. The integrity of the system of contribution and co-operation repairs itself and evolves. Democracy is founded on co-operation and contribution.

So, the integrity of the system of human evolution requires co-operation and contribution. Let's now take this a step further and look at integrity from an ethical point of view. In ethics, integrity is regarded as the honesty and truthfulness or accuracy of one's actions. We can see the sociopath fails when it comes to integrity, but this usually comes back to bite them in one way or another. We can also see the lack of integrity in our political systems and politicians. Even systems that are supposed to be democratic have politicians that lie and manipulate for power. A lie has its roots in the want for control. Deception has its roots in the want for control. Stealing is a want for approval, control and security.

To see what others have and what we have not is a temptation to want more - at whatever cost.

As my father looked out of the window, he commented, 'I am surprised there is a tree left in Flimby Wood with all the walking sticks in Maryport' (my birthplace). His comment was based on the number of people walking past with walking sticks tucked under their arms while marching down the street to the pub - all claiming the disability pension. I was taken back to that moment a year ago on a visit back to my home town. A friend from the past was telling me he had now retired on a disability pension and life was good. Later that night, I noticed his walking stick against the wall as he rocked and rolled with his wife across the dance floor, putting guys half his age to shame. The imbalance in wealth in society will often create a retreat from ethical choices just to survive with a more comfortable life. *To see what others have and what we have not is a temptation to want more - at whatever cost.* Sometimes that cost is our integrity.

Let's take a look at religion as a basis for ethical behaviour. We can look at the Ten Commandments and the Buddha's Eight-fold path for this. I am not religious but there are valid lessons to learn here.

Ethics

Ethics and the Ten Commandments.

We can see that commandments five through to ten have their base in ethics and integrity.

5: Honour your father and your mother.

6: You shall not murder.

7: You shall not commit adultery.

8: You shall not steal.

9: You shall not bear false witness against your neighbour.

10: You shall not covet your neighbour's house; you shall not covet your neighbour's wife, nor his male servant, nor his female servant, nor his ox, nor his donkey, nor anything that is your neighbour's.

(I don't know about you but I am certainly not about to covet my neighbours ass!)

Ethics and the Buddha's Eight Fold Path.

If we look at the three areas under ethical conduct we can see the basis of living with integrity. Areas three through to five.

3: Right Speech

4: Right Action

5: Right Livelihood

Right Speech

The focus of the Right Speech is to avoid harmful language, such as lying or unkind words. It is far better to use gentle, friendly and meaningful words, even when a situation calls for a truth that may be hurtful, despite the follower's best intentions.

Right Action

The Right Action forms a list of fundamental ethical behaviours all practising Buddhists should follow. These are the Five Precepts:

To refrain from destroying living beings
To refrain from stealing
To refrain from sexual misconduct (adultery, rape, etc.)
To refrain from false speech (lying)
To refrain from intoxicants which lead to heedlessness.

Right Livelihood

Those seeking enlightenment should pick the Right Livelihood to support the other fundamentals of Buddhism. Followers should avoid employment in positions where their actions may cause harm to others, be it directly or indirectly.

Here we can see how the ethics in the eight fold path follow the ethics in the last five Commandments and also that these ethics have a base in system integrity – co-operation and contribution. *Right action, right speech, and right livelihood are the basis of integrity.*

I also find it interesting that the second commandment is similar to what the Buddha said. You shall not make for yourself a carved image - any likeness of anything that is in heaven above, or that is in the earth beneath, or that is in the water under the earth. How many images do you see in a Christian church or Buddhist temple? It makes them sectarian and I tend to think this was the reason why it was suggested that images should not be worshiped. It is the principles, not the image, which we need to embody. *The image is nothing more than imagination and can be distorted – the principles can be tested for truth.* A principle is a foundation upon which other values and measures of integrity are based.

If we live our lives through these principles, we meet our needs and the needs of others. We have integrity and the system maintains integrity. We continue to evolve. If we don't, we frustrate our needs and the needs of others. We fail to evolve. The universe doesn't discriminate. It appears to be an elegant system that seems to have a built-in safety mechanism that eliminates all who don't adapt to its changing conditions and evolve. Integrity follows the rules of cause and effect, chaos and stability.

Sociopathic tendencies may well be genetic but may also be learned - the ego's effort to protect the heart from pain and in so doing to harden it. Many criminals show remorse and learn lessons from a lack of integrity. They transform their lives into something better. A lack of integrity will always offer lessons to learn. If you don't learn the lesson you are doomed to repeat it.

There is a Prime Minister of Australia at who promised before an election, never to bring in a carbon tax under the government she led. Without this promise she would never have been elected. Once in power she moved to bring in a carbon tax, a deal made with other parties and so called independent politicians seeking increased power. This lack of integrity created a massive slide in her approval. It had nothing to do with a carbon tax. Most people understand the need to reduce pollution. The rejection of her was all to do with the lie to gain power at all costs - the lack of integrity. Trust is a connecting habit. If we feel we can't trust someone we feel disconnected and disempowered. It is one of the reasons why politicians are the least trusted people in society. They far too often sacrifice honesty and integrity for power. I find it interesting that we don't usually say 'those in government,' we usually say 'those in power.' I also find it laughable that politicians call each other the *right honourable member* - nothing honourable in a lack of integrity.

We have integrity when we see ourselves as part of the whole.

The word *integrity* stems from the Latin adjective *integer* (whole, complete). In the context of wholeness, integrity is the inner sense of *wholeness* deriving from qualities such as honesty and consistency of character. We have integrity when we see ourselves as part of the whole. We lack integrity when we are stuck in this limited and tiny *I, me and mine* of the ego - stuck in wanting and not giving. Respecting the individual rights of others to meet their needs is the first step to having integrity.

The old saying, 'do unto others as you would have them do unto you' might be a good place to start.

Don't bother too much about the problems created by the egos of others. Karma would seem to be the basic universal law of cause and effect in action. It usually catches up on a person one way or another. They become victims of themselves. Accept that the system of integrity must win out at some time in the future and go with the flow - with an acceptance and an allowance of things. We can now see that with conscious choice comes responsibility; our ability to respond - to make a choice. What are you choosing? Are you choosing actions that have integrity or actions that lack integrity? This will determine how happy you are, whether you know it or not! Actions that come from a place of integrity may not give you what you want. They will give you what you need!

The purpose of a good business is to provide a service to the community and, in doing so, make a profit for its shareholders. Many businesses lose sight of this as top executives focus on maximising profits and their personal remuneration – not their service to the customer or the community in general.

The purpose of Government is to provide for the basic needs of the community – education, food, shelter, health and freedom from harm. It should provide basic resources and an environment where people can contribute and co-operate. Politicians are public servants. They should be serving the public not dictating to them.

The blunt truth is not always in your best interests. If my wife asks if her bottom looks big in the dress she has tried on I will always say no. Why? If my wife likes her dress I don't want to spoil her happiness. Have I lost my integrity by saying this? If we look back to co-operation and contribution we can see that honesty is not a blunt instrument. It can be withdrawn if it hurts no one and causes no harm. The man told he has a serious illness may not tell the full truth to his family. It is designed to stop hurt rather than to deceive to cause hurt.

CHAPTER SIXTEEN

Understanding the Bully

 *The bully feels like a victim and tries to make a victim of others.*

Here is an old rhyme from when I was a kid. 'sticks and stones may break my bones but words can never hurt me.'

Most verbal bullying comes in the form of disconnecting habits of communication. *This is external control psychology* as covered by William Glasser. They are, criticizing, complaining, threatening, blaming, nagging, punishing and bribing. The bullies feel disconnected and disempowered in their lives, and attack others to control them. In so doing, feel they have some sense of power. It's a knife that cuts both ways. It hurts the bully just as much as the one being bullied. This is the ego at its worst but, unlike the sociopath, the bully feels like a victim and tries to make a victim of others.

We take being bullied personally. It isn't personal. It's the bully's problem. They are the ones that feel powerless. If they didn't feel powerless they wouldn't need to bully others. If we don't take it personally we can't be bullied verbally. We should feel sorry for the bully. They don't live happy lives, poor things. Sociopaths are effective bullies. This comes from a hidden sense of rage that they have supressed and a lack of guilt or remorse.

The bully lives in fear, stuck in the mind. From the heart we can feel compassion for the poor souls and this frees us. There is another thing about bullies. They have usually been bullied in the past. It takes a bully to create a bully. They have low self-esteem and will usually target the weak to feel strong. The paradox is that they must feel weak to want to feel strong. Because of low self-esteem the ego wants to inflate itself to feel superior to others - again a paradox. You must feel inferior to others to want to feel superior to them and you must feel powerless to want power over others. Bullies often recruit others who feel weak to help them bully. This is often the choice; better to be on the side of the bully than to be bullied by them. Most bullies are cowards who live in fear.

Many parents bully their children without even knowing they are doing it. Many bosses bully staff at work thinking they are just doing their job. Once we realise that the disconnecting habits are our bullying behaviour, we can make amends. We have all been guilty of it at some time or other.

Many parents who were punished as children believe that, if it worked for them, it will work for their children. If we don't punish our children they won't learn what they are doing wrong. Punishment is a disconnecting habit. There is a simple tool I teach to clients to avoid using this disconnecting habit. I have the parents sit down with their children and come up with a set of rules they all agree on. The parents then negotiate the consequences of their children breaking these rules. Once a child accepts the negotiated consequence they are taking ownership of the consequence. If they break the rules it isn't the parent dishing out the punishment. They are punishing themselves. When the parent punishes a child, the child feels as though they are being bullied. If the child has agreed to the consequences of breaking the rules they must understand that they have a choice. Allowing a child to have a choice meets that child's need for empowerment. No one is trying to take their power away. If a child misbehaves, the parent just needs to point out the consequence that they have mutually chosen. The behaviour eventually stops because there is no battle between the parent's ego and the child's.

I find children will test the parent's resolve in following through with the consequences. The child has chosen the consequences so there is no need for the parent to feel guilty about following through with them. I find that this helps a child understand that there are consequences to all their actions. This is a good lesson to learn at an early age.

The following is an example from a client's feedback. The lady in question came to me because she was stressed and frustrated with her two young children's behaviour. She had resorted to shouting at them all the time, and punishing them didn't seem to work. They had become worse.

I think when some children hear, 'don't do that' from a parent, the 'don't' seems to get deleted. They don't like to be told what to do. Telling is a disconnecting habit.

The mother sat her children down, a boy six years old and a girl of five. There were some of her children's behaviours creating problems for her. She wanted to stop these behaviours. They were fighting each other, not getting ready for school on time and her son was jumping on the furniture – and there was more. She had them agree that rules were fair and necessary. She then negotiated the consequences of this behaviour with each of them. The example she gave me was her son jumping on the furniture. The consequence would be the confiscation of his playstation. The boy wanted 1 day loss and she wanted a week. They settled on five days. The next day he was again jumping on the furniture. She didn't shout at him as she would normally have done. She just asked him if he was choosing to lose his playstation. He jumped off. As soon as her back was turned he jumped back on. She began to pack up his playstation as he protested that it wasn't fair. She told him she wasn't punishing him. He had chosen it and was punishing himself. He tried to get it back a few days later but she stayed consistent for the five days. The behaviour stopped shortly after.

The son was clever in the negotiations. He had asked for rules for his mother. He said he didn't like it when she shouted at him all the time. They agreed that if she shouted at them she would sit in the naughty corner for one hour. This was a chair in the laundry. She was confident that now she had a strategy in place there was no need to shout and so agreed. A few weeks later they were late in getting ready for school in time and she shouted at them, forgetting the consequences she had agreed to. The son quickly pointed this out and the consequence. She agreed to accept the consequence after she picked them up from school. 'One hour is a long time with two young children sitting cross legged on the floor giggling', she told me. She also told me she had learned a lesson of her own that day. Sometimes old habits take time to break. Sometimes parents don't understand the consequences of their own actions, but will eventually pay a price one way or another.

When we use disconnecting habits we are trying to control others.

When we use disconnecting habits on others. It is bullying. As children we take it personally. As adults we can choose to take it personally. It isn't personal. It is the other person's problem so we don't need to take it personally. Some parents are still bullying their children long after they have grown into adults. Some parents still feel the need to control their children regardless of their age. They love their children but create problems in their relationship by trying to control them.

One of the best words you can use to yourself if someone is using disconnecting habits is – *interesting*. Interesting places us in the position of the observer. If you find the bully's comments interesting, you are not taking them personally. Only the ego takes it personally. When I find a bully's comments interesting, it takes me to a place of wondering what their problem is.

Some bullies have passive-aggressive behaviour. These are the hard ones to pick. They tell you what you want to hear and then do something else. They can't say it to your face but work behind your back. To your face they never utter an unpleasant word, but, as they are walking out the door, their fiendish minds are working on a plot to bring you down or disrupt your plans, your suggestions or directions. Most passive-aggressive people feel insecure.

Passive-aggressive behaviour is a learned personality trait. Their passive, sometimes obstructionist resistance to following through with expectations in interpersonal or occupational situations can cause many problems. It is a personality trait marked by a pervasive pattern of negative attitudes and passive, usually disavowed, resistance in interpersonal or occupational situations. It can manifest itself as a learned helplessness, procrastination, stubbornness, resentment, sullenness, or deliberate and repeated failure to accomplish requested tasks. The passive-aggressive persons sees themselves as the victim of bullying – but they try to bully others by their actions. Passive-aggressive people like to gossip. It is often a result of a problem with a parent in childhood or bullying, but it is a learned behavior and usually a sad sign of immaturity. Some passive-aggressive behaviours are designed to push your buttons to help to make them feel superior, but to avoid a reaction. One passive-aggressive person I know will often suggest, that people who think a certain way, or act a certain way are idiots. While knowing full well it's the way I would probably think or act. You know it's aimed at you but it is a comment designed to hurt and yet avoid conflict. I find it interesting that he needs to try to pull me and others down through generalized judgmental comments to feel good. Like all bullies, he wants to feel superior, but must feel inferior to behave this way. I also find it sad because he is usually a very nice guy. It is designed to inflict pain, and yet avoid conflict. Once a passive-aggressive person decides not to like you, there is not much you can do to change it. They will tell you what you want to hear to your face, but you don't want to hear what they say behind your back. Their actions or lack of, are designed to frustrate you.

Most bullies are made - not born that way. They were created by circumstance. Cut them some slack and don't take it personally - It's their problem, not yours.

CHAPTER SEVENTEEN

Christ was not a Christian, Buddha was not a Buddhist.

Religion brings many benefits but causes many problems.

Seven years ago, and before moving into psychotherapy, I attended a 10 day, live in Vipassana meditation course. I was feeling stressed with the politics being played out at work and had already decided to leave the company and focus on my studies in psychotherapy. It was done on a whim. I had web-searched for a course and what interested me was the fact that you didn't have to pay. You could donate at the end of the course if you could afford to or wanted to, but it was not a requirement for attending the course. I found that centres had sprung up all over the world and all were paid for through donations, and everyone helping on the course was a volunteer. I also liked the idea that we were not allowed to speak for the full ten days. I was 'talked-out' and wanted some space.

The course was secular, which was good because I had no belief in God. At an early age my parents, (father a Catholic and mother a Protestant) made a point of not pushing me into religion. I remember being hit by a nun with a walking stick for playing football on the Catholic football field and chastised by a vicar for playing in the church grounds. If these were God's representatives I thought there couldn't be a God. This lack of belief was helped along by the war in Ireland between the Catholics and Protestants (although being pulled out of school because of a bomb scare and sent home was a joy I looked forward to!) The British have been so pillaged and plundered by the Vikings, Romans, French and Germans over the years that no-one seemed much bothered about the odd bomb threat. We were just lined up in an orderly fashion and marched to the front yard before a roll call and then despatched home. On this ten day meditation course my lack of belief in something more would be challenged.

I sat cross legged on the floor for the first meditation session. We were told to focus on the breath, as it passed back and forth through the nostrils, with our eyes closed. That lasted all of twenty seconds then the mind wandered off for a few minutes before being caught and returned for another twenty seconds. It was not as easy as I thought it would be, with the mind jumping like a mad monkey from tree to tree. The second thing I noticed was my foot going numb and my ankle and back beginning to ache. Ten minutes in and I was beginning to doubt my ability to stay the course. Each hour we would break and limp out into the sunshine on numb feet wondering what we had got ourselves into. I decided that, if I got through the first six days, I would make the ten. Over the subsequent days my focus became more concentrated and my mind wandered less; but the pain didn't abate. I would long for the end of each hour. DVDs and CDs taught the technique and the reasons for it. At the end of the one hour session the CD would spring to life with a minute of talking. There was a sense of relief as the CD kicked into life but that minute seemed to go on forever. By day four, a strange thing started to happen. I could feel sensations all the way around my nostrils and through my nose. It felt like my nose was getting bigger and growing out of my face. I would check the mirror between sessions but it didn't look any different. We were asked if we had experienced any nasal sensations and yes, we had.

Day five continued in the same painful way. I was limping in and out between sessions and hoping I hadn't permanently damaged something. But then a new technique was introduced. We began to focus on the top of the head and become aware of the sensations there. Once the sensations were felt at the top of the head, we moved in steps down through our bodies until we reached those aching knees and feet. Now here was the trick; we had to observe the sensations throughout the body with equanimity, not good or bad, not with a craving for the good sensations or an aversion to the uncomfortable sensations. Well, believe me. I had an aversion to what I was feeling in my back, knees and feet. I was in pain. My little western body was used to sitting in a nice comfortable chair. It might be okay for some guy from India 2500 years ago when there might not have been too many chairs around, but I had spent nearly fifty years in comfortable chairs with back rests. I was definitely feeling an aversion to the pain.

I persisted and eventually began to feel pleasant sensations running through my body. I found this interesting. I was becoming aware of more sensations both subtle and gross: (gross sensations can be pain, discomfort or dull thick sensations). The end of day six came with great relief. For the first time I was confident of finishing the ten days. I retired to bed that night feeling quite proud of myself and decided to meditate while on my back before I slept. It was much more comfortable than sitting cross legged and in pain. Soon the cascading sensations could be felt throughout the body but there seemed to be a higher vibration to them and these vibrations seemed to be getting faster and stronger - almost pulsing. It seemed more pronounced - in my head, hands and feet. There seemed to be a cascading flicker of lights beneath my eyelids like Roman candle fireworks. The last thought I remember having was, 'just join the dots,' meaning the vibrations in the head, hands and feet. And then zap. The thoughts stopped. Time stopped and I was no longer aware of my body. There are no words to describe the experience because it was beyond mind and body, but I will try. Pure bliss and a feeling of pure love, and it seemed like I was basking in a golden glow. At that instant, I felt a sense of knowing of some higher intelligence: of some higher power; something more than the little me; a quantum consciousness, a feeling of pure love and acceptance: something I can't describe. Call it what you will - Nirvana - a state of non-suffering – non-duality - you can't describe the indescribable. Try to describe the taste of an apple. It can't be described in words: only experienced.

I still find the word *God* not the easiest to roll off my lips. In that moment, I felt that I knew that I was a part of something, but I can't explain what - and it was a part of me - there was no separation. I also had a strong sense that there is eternal life, or maybe it was a sense of no past and no future, just an eternal now. I find it difficult to put into words. I also had a sense of understanding the perfection of all that is happening in the material world. No thoughts, no words - just a sense of knowing. Maybe I was just experiencing a higher level of consciousness - a mind devoid of conditioned fear. I can understand how some might attribute this type of experience to God realisation. I don't see it as a religious experience - just an experience that left more questions than it gave answers. I don't know how long it lasted but I knew I couldn't stay there, and back I came. The first thought was 'now I know why people meditate.' I drifted off to sleep looking forward to the next day. I thought I had it sussed. I was up by 4:00am and quickly off to the meditations hall looking to quickly get back to that place. I was soon disappointed. My mind was pouring forth thoughts that I have never experienced before: that my wife was having an affair with my daughter's friend's father. That was impossible. That friends and work colleagues were working behind my back. I had never felt so negative and aggravated. I couldn't even focus on my breathing for ten seconds without the mind spewing up more rubbish. I was ready to quit. You could talk to the instructor at lunch time if you were having problems and so off I went to see him. I told him of the experience from the night before and he said I had experienced 'samadi.' Touching the toe in the river of enlightenment is the way he described it. I told him I wanted it back and he smiled. 'Craving the good feelings?' he asked.

'I just want to get it back', I said.

'And the more you crave it the more you push it away,' he said. That's just what I didn't want to hear.

'But what about all this negative stuff coming up?' I asked him.

'You have opened up the subconscious and the defilements of the mind are pouring forth. If you can look at them with equanimity they will pass and be eradicated. This is of more benefit than the bliss: an opportunity to cleanse the mind', he said. Not the answers I wanted.

I stayed and finished the ten days - the rubbish coming up slowly subsided - but no more bliss. I couldn't deny my experience, but still don't like the word 'God' to explain it. I felt I was in the knowing of something I could no longer deny, and it wasn't some little old man sitting up in the clouds judging everyone. It was indescribable, and that knowing has never left me. And the sense of knowing about being eternal has totally changed my thinking about death. What I did lose was any knowing or sensing of any perfection of it all. I could see no perfection in a child dying of hunger, or someone being murdered. That part of the experience was left behind. It was a number of years before I could get close to that experience again and I have still not fully experienced it again in its totality. I have come close to it, but I have stopped chasing it; stopped craving it. I still try to meditate each day and see it as a process of evolution.

I now look at religion through different eyes. I see the Buddha mind and Christ consciousness as the same things taught in different ways but leading the way to the same outcome - eradication of the ego mind to find the true essence of what we are. Buddha was not a Buddhist! Siddhattha Gotama was a man who achieved the Buddha mind: the enlightened mind that no longer sees reality through the filter of the ego. Christ was a man called Jesus, who probably became Christ at his point of enlightenment. Both these men taught basically the same things: non-violence and love and compassion for your fellow man. Both were egoless and full of humility, love and compassion. The Buddha didn't call it 'God realisation' probably because there were so many gods in the other religions going around at the time. He taught a philosophy of training the mind to reach Nirvana - a supreme state of non-suffering. One God was probably a more acceptable way of bringing the teachings to life in Christ's time.

In many religions the teachers' teachings have been distorted by man's egos.

How many people have died in the name of God and how many crimes have been committed in the name of God? The ego likes to believe that its god is better than anyone else's god. In many religions the teachers' teachings have been distorted by man's egos and the resultant desire to control other people. It's no wonder that religion has lost its flavour for so many, when we see so many acts of brutality committed in the name of God. The basics of most religions are as valid today as they were thousands of years ago: simply tools to help us to evolve into all we can be. I didn't have to be a Buddhist to experience what I experienced. I just used the tools set out so many years ago. We can be told something and intellectually we can understand it, but true knowledge only comes from the experience of it.

There can be no wars fought on religious principles that do not break the basic principles of their teachings.

Christ was not a Christian, he was Jewish. He just didn't meet the criteria to be the Jewish messiah and so was rejected by the Jews. Christianity started sixty years after he died.

In churches, Christ looks like the epitome of a movie star - tall and good looking. Just the sort of image that God says we shouldn't have, if we adhere to the Ten Commandments. There is a good chance he looked more like Woody Allen - short, balding and with a big nose. (And I would hope enlightened beings and Woody Allen would have a good sense of humour or I could be in serious trouble.) The Buddha is seen in temples around the world as sometimes fat, sometimes thin. What are we to believe? Didn't he care about his diet or health? Let's face it; the overweight image is not an ideal role model for a healthy life! Being overweight was often a sign of being successful in some cultures and in times when food was short. There were no cameras around at that time. Was he worshiping Hindu Gods before his enlightenment? Why was he overweight if he had no cravings? Who knows? We do know that what Christ and Buddha taught had an impact on so many people and still does today – but how much of this comes from them, and how much from the ego of the people that followed - not quite that enlightened? The images they might have created could have been to control us. I am not trying here to besmirch the image or teachings of Christ or Buddha. Their basic teachings have stood the test of time and are as true today as they were then. I am only trying to point out that we need to find the truth of reality within ourselves. And isn't that exactly what they taught? *Principles are more important than the fabricated images. The principles that they taught were supposed to unite men - never to divide.* There can be no wars fought on religious principles that do not break the basic principles of their teachings.

CHAPTER EIGHTEEN

Culture and Morale

Co-operation and contribution can overcome cultural differences.

Cultural differences are the result of our conditioning. The culture of a people is a direct result of the conditioning of the people around them. Many cultural differences come from different belief systems formed by this conditioning. Interaction between different cultures results in an expansion of both. Often the opposite is also true. What should be assimilation often turns to alienation because of our conflicting beliefs. Most conflict comes from rigid religious or racial beliefs.

I was born in England and have lived most my life in Australia. I worked for months at a time in China and Thailand. I have worked in America, Denmark, Holland, New Zealand and elsewhere. I have worked in every state in Australia and have found differing cultures in all places. The culture in the city is different to rural culture in all these places and each place is different to the other. I have worked for a number of different companies and the culture of one organisation can be greatly different to another.

What is normal? Nothing! What seems normal to one person seems abnormal to another. It is often difficult to understand others from our own limited cultural belief system. No two people have the same life experiences or are exposed to the same cultural beliefs. There can be similarities based on similar beliefs. But different personalities and life experiences will create different belief systems. No two people can see the world in the identical way. We are all looking at the world through a different set of filters. Even people from the same family will have different belief systems.

When we are looking at a cultural belief system we are looking at a dominant set of beliefs of that culture. These dominant sets will vary from culture to culture. Some cultures are similar and some seem poles apart.

There are some basic elements to integrating cultures. Co-operation and contribution are the foundation on which all else sits. Co-operation allows for the different belief systems of others. Respect (which is a part of co-operation) is not imposing your own beliefs on others and the individual rights of others. We all have the same genetic needs and co-operation and contribution to society meet those needs. Respecting the laws and rules of the culture you are in is the foundation for integration.

I wrote earlier about how human beings survived through learning to adapt. When you enter a country with a different culture to the one in which you were born, learning to adapt to this culture makes for happiness. You must adapt to integrate. Adaptation enables integration. Integration facilitates acceptance. Many Greeks and Italians have migrated to Australia, bringing with them a culture rich in food and wine. The British probably introduced fish and chips and beer, the staple diet of my teenage years! This has enhanced the Australian culture by adding to it. We now have a culture rich with all the foods of the world. The contribution and co-operation of new migrants helped build

Australia into the country that it is today. New immigrants adapted to new laws and rules and yet at the same time they could enhance the culture of this country by adding to it. Elements of their culture enhance the new culture.

Another thing I like about the culture of Australia is the culture of volunteering time for worthy causes, for the greater community. Every junior sporting club is filled with such volunteers. This is probably the reason why we fare so well in sport despite our small population. This is where we see co-operation and contribution coming together to create a culture that benefits all.

 *If the culture of an organisation is one of fear, this will spread like a cancer through the organisation and result in poor morale.*

In business the culture of one organisation can be vastly different to another. Often the culture of an organisation is determined by the management. In some organisations people are treated like people. In other organisations people are treated like dispensable numbers. This is often transferred into the way they treat their customers, resulting in poor customer service. Profit numbers are often becoming more important than providing a service to the community or developing a positive culture in a company. If the culture of an organisation is one of fear, this will spread like a cancer through the organisation and result in poor morale. If the culture is based on co-operation and contribution this culture will flourish and so will the company. In a company with a culture based on co-operation and contribution, profit will follow like the cart follows the horse. The culture of a company is also reflected in the morale of the people working for it. One person in a position of management can create poor morale in an organisation through disconnecting habits. The boss manager doesn't promote a culture of co-operation and contribution. They create a culture of disconnection and disempowerment and poor morale follows.

We often see managers who believe they are at the top of the tree but who are only making decisions for the benefit of themselves. Good management realises it begins at the bottom of the tree - the roots that feed the tree to help it flourish. They are the foundation on which the tree grows. There are times when dead branches need to be pruned for the tree to remain healthy. When the roots feed the tree, co-operation and contribution is nature at work. The roots need the branches and leaves and the branches and leaves need the roots. Both are interdependent for the tree to survive and grow. There is no separation and none is more important than the other - just as every cell in the body is required to serve its purpose. What purpose? Contribution and co-operation - integrating as part of the whole and not believing it is separate from the whole.

Everyone can do their bit to improve the culture of a country, a business or even a family through co-operation and contribution. It needs to start with each of us to influence the rest.

CHAPTER NINETEEN

Forgiveness

Forgiveness frees the forgiver as well as the forgiven.

We have all been hurt by people in the past. Holding onto this hurt keeps us in the past and always a victim of the perpetrator. To forgive is not that easy and will often be rejected as not an option, but it is a choice. How can you forgive someone who abuses a child or rapes someone, or a person who kills another, or someone who steals from you and gets away with it?

These perpetrators and predators are the true losers in life. They could never be happy to commit these crimes in the first place and could never be happy after committing them. They are their own worst enemies. Stuck in the worst of their ego selves they create drama, and as a consequence that drama will be returned eventually. Sick and sad people are what they are, never to be happy. That's karma: they are victims of themselves. Forgiveness is about taking your power back. Getting back the power that was taken from you. Why should you feel bad when you have done nothing wrong?

A young girl was sexually abused by her grandfather at the age of eight. He was on holiday staying with her family. He had entered her bedroom one night after a party at her parents' place. Her shouts brought her mother. He had no business being there but denied he had done anything wrong. The father was told by his wife's sister that it was probably just a nightmare. This created just enough doubt for the father to withdraw from retribution. The grandfather was told that under the circumstances he could no longer stay.

The following day the accusations began to fly. It must be the girl seeking attention because the father often worked overseas, and was not around as often as he should be. The sisters never spoke to each other again. The father lost a good friend in his brother-in-law. The mother's only contact for many years from her own mother was letters telling her how this had destroyed her family, and how her husband could never have done such a thing. In counselling, the girl's mother was told her daughter could not describe what had happened in such detail if it had not in fact happened.

The girl's mother and grandmother's relationship was suffering and so it was decided to build a bridge. Nothing was mentioned again about the incident. The grandparents would come from overseas for holidays but would stay in the parents holiday cabin. The young girl who was now a teenager would not have to see her grandfather and didn't want to. She could stay at home.

When she was twenty-seven with her own house and two children, it was proposed that her grandparents would come and stay in the family home with her parents. She had a problem with this. Her parents looked after her two sons on Mondays when she worked. She didn't like the idea of her grandfather being around them. It was decided that they could be looked after by someone else during this time. She was still stressing and didn't know why. She came to me for counselling.

I told her that until she forgave him she would always be his victim. She didn't want to forgive him. That would be like letting him get away with what he had done. He had caused her years of torment. I told her that I couldn't forgive him for her and asked her how long she was willing to hold on to this. How long was she willing to be his victim? I said that he was a victim of himself. He had fractured his family and caused so much hurt. I told her that he could deny it to everyone else, but he knew that she knew what he had done. He couldn't escape that fact.

The day after they arrived she called to say she was bringing her family to see them. She walked in and hugged her grandmother and then her grandfather. He broke down and cried. He never admitted anything, and nothing was mentioned.

It takes courage to forgive - to let go of the hurt.

She told me afterwards it was like a heavy weight being lifted from her shoulders. She knew he couldn't hurt her anymore and felt sorry for him. He was still her grandfather. At the end of their stay he told the girl's father that it had been the best two weeks of his life. It seems as though a weight had been lifted off his shoulders. He died within three months of returning home.

You don't need to give the perpetrator a hug or talk to them to forgive. This was done in the above case to heal the family's pain and put an end to it, but she also did it for herself, not for him. In most cases it would be best to avoid any contact with the perpetrator whatsoever. Some might have long since died or been imprisoned. They are all prisoners of their past actions and all losers because of these actions. I don't want to be the victim of a loser.

It takes courage to forgive - to let go of the hurt. The ego wants us to hold onto it. It thrives on being a victim. It only exists if we are victims. The biggest barrier to forgiving is the feeling of the injustice of it all. It isn't fair. However, bad things happen to good people. It is just a fact of life. Where egos abound there will be injustice. The more a person allows their ego to run the show, the more they will hurt others and be hurt. The ego of a person can always rationalise its reason for hurting others and the person will deny they are at fault. The person stuck in their ego hurts themselves as much as they hurt anyone else without even realising it. It's a knife that cuts both ways.

It is hard to forgive a bully without understanding their behaviour. Understanding that the bully must feel powerless, disconnected and disempowered to act the way they do can be the first step to dropping the injustice we feel.

Our reputation is in the hands of others. We have no control over it. Our character is in our own hands, no one can touch it. I have seen many good people have their reputations trashed by colleagues looking to further their own self-interests. Sometimes we need to forgive and forget. Sometimes we need to forgive but not forget. Often we need to remember the type of person we are dealing with to protect ourselves from further harm. If we understand that the person doing the harm to us is doing it from their own place of suffering and creating more suffering for themselves, we can forgive from a point of compassion for the loser that they are and feel sorry for them, which is in turn a form of compassion. Sometimes we just need to say *stuff them*. They are just idiots and losers and I don't want to lose myself to them any longer. I am taking my power back.'

The greatest gift we can give ourselves is the gift of forgiveness. Only by choosing to forgive can we be truly free of the past and no longer victims of it.

CHAPTER TWENTY

Is there a Law of Attraction?

Love is the true law of attraction.

I was always of the opinion that what we bring into our world is the result of our thinking and, in turn, action - cause and effect. There is much said these days about the law of attraction - the universe rearranging itself as a result of what we hold in our minds, or the thoughts we put out. The biggest problem I had with this concept was just how could you prove it?

Cellular Biologist Bruce Lipton, in his book *Biology of Belief,* answered a few questions for me with regard to this. He states in his book that quantum physicists have discovered that physical atoms are made of vortices of energy that are constantly spinning and vibrating. Each atom has its own specific energy signature and assemblies of atoms and molecules, collectively radiate their own identifying energy patterns. He suggests that every material structure in the universe including each of us human beings has its own unique energy structure. So, atoms are made up of invisible energy not tangible matter. Quantum physics reveals that the universe is an integration of interdependent energy fields that are interwoven in a network of interactions. Further, Bruce Lipton states that our thoughts and subconscious beliefs are also energy that will have an effect on our body at a cellular level. His book is well worth a read.

Working as a psychotherapist, and using clinical hypnotherapy to change limiting beliefs at a subconscious level, this just made sense to me. I was taught, and have accepted through experience, that the subconscious belief system is the root cause of many of our problems, both mental and often physical. We can now understand how a person unknowingly taking a placebo (sugar pill) can bring positive results to their health through only the use of the belief system.

If this universe is an integration of interdependent energy fields that are interwoven in a mesh of interactions, then it would make sense that thoughts and beliefs might also affect what is going on outside the body as well as inside the body. The following story about a client turned my old thinking as to the law of attraction upside down.

A fifty six year old woman came to see me one day. She had booked an appointment for hypnotherapy. She told me that at the age of seventeen she was living in Perth. She had met a man and become pregnant. She became afraid of a possible lack of support being away from home, and returned to Melbourne to be with her family where she gave birth to a baby girl. Two years later she discovered the child's father was living in Adelaide and took her daughter to meet him. He wanted her to stay but again, feeling afraid and insecure, she left. He was living with another woman at the time. She hadn't seen him since that day. She thought it was time her daughter got to meet her father and was trying to track him down. All she could find, even using a private detective, was that someone thought they had seen him at Sydney Casino two years earlier. She gave me his name and said he was of Maltese decent and older than she. She also mentioned he liked to gamble. She then asked me to try to uncover forgotten memories from that time, his date of birth etc. through hypnosis.

I must admit I wasn't confident a regression would bring up anything of value. While under hypnosis she wouldn't go back to that point in time - she said it was too painful. She also said she realised she had other issues to deal with and wanted to continue therapy to resolve these. She told me she knew she would find him but thought she must have been drawn to see me for a different reason. We resolved her issues over the next few months. Mid-way through the sessions she came in one day quite happy and said she was off to Sydney at the weekend with her daughter to find him. I asked if the private detective had come up with anything and she said *no*. But she said she knew she would find him. I expected she and her daughter would have a nice weekend away together but I thought it would be impossible to find him.

At the following week's appointment she came in smiling. I asked how the weekend had gone and was told she had found him on the first day. She then happily went on to produce photographs of the three of them together on the weekend. I asked how she had found him and she said; *I just knew I would.* I knew then that there had been no doubt in her mind. No fear of not finding him. My first thought was how could this be possible? I sat amazed as she told me of the weekend away.

They had travelled to Sydney and gone straight to the Casino - the last place she thought he had been seen two years earlier. They looked around for a few hours before asking a worker there if he knew of an area in Sydney where Maltese people might congregate. She was told about a strip of coffee shops. Heading off to this area she proceeded to go from coffee shop to coffee shop asking if they knew of anyone with his name. At one coffee shop she was told that someone with that first name came in but wasn't that regular although he had been that morning - they didn't know his second name. She asked if there was a gambling place close by and was told there was a betting shop around the corner.

Walking in to the betting shop she turned to her daughter and said 'that's your dad walking into the toilets.' She recognised him from the back. Her daughter said she wasn't going to stand around while her mother made a fool of herself and went for a coffee. When he returned from the toilet he was talking to someone who noticed her looking at him and mentioned it to him. He turned around and went white as a sheet. She said to him 'I have brought your daughter to meet you.'

He was now sixty one and married with two grown children. She was fifty six and her daughter was thirty nine. They hadn't seen or heard from each other for thirty seven years and she had recognised him from the back. He had been twenty one when they met and twenty three the last time they saw each other. The other interesting thing is that he had spent most of these years in Melbourne, not that far from where she lived.

What were the odds of finding him? Sydney has a population of over 4.5 million people. He could have been in Perth, Adelaide, Melbourne or Sydney. He could have been living in a country town or outer suburbs. A lot of people don't live until they are sixty. How many coffee shops and betting shops are there in Sydney? The list and the odds go on. She found him in less than six hours. I doubt that even the police, with his name and approximate age and a range of sophisticated computers, could have accomplished this. I would have thought she would have had more chance of winning the lotto three weeks in a row than of finding him in less than six hours!

Is there a law of attraction? Some who push this law of attraction theory say you need to hold in your mind what you want to attract - but isn't a want a fear of lack? Surely you will be left lacking? If there is a law of attraction (and I am not sure there is) it is the knowing without doubt - the belief that creates it. Let me try it now. I *know* this book will be published and I *know* you will be reading it. Did it work?

It is an interesting thought: an elegant, intelligent universe and we are all co-creators in it. I can't say if the above story is proof of the law of attraction or just remarkable coincidence. I can say that every breath you take is a gift of life to be cherished. You would not be bothered with the trivial things in life with just one breath to go. We enter this world with nothing and leave with nothing. All you really leave behind is a footprint of the love you have given – this is your legacy and it lives on long after you have gone. If you live life through your heart with love and compassion for others it will be returned ten-fold. This is what you will attract. Whose life is richer? A man with his heart filled with love or a man with his pocket filled with coin? I doubt that a man on his deathbed would be wishing he had more money in the bank. He might be wishing he had more love in his life - when it is all too late. It costs nothing to love now and love is something you can only give, not get. In giving love you attract love (You can prove this law of attraction!) It then returns with abundance. If there is a universal law of attraction then let love be your priority. If we all focused on this, what a wonderful world it would be. All material things are really immaterial in comparison to love. A person living with love and compassion for others is truly the most attractive person of all - and probably the happiest and therefore the most successful. I think by now you will understand that a life without some sort of ethical and moral discipline will not be a happy life. Through an ethical moral life you meet your needs. Without it you will frustrate them. Life is not easy, it takes courage to be strong in what is right and wrong. Being strong in what you want is not being strong in what you need. It is a small point but makes an enormous difference in your perspective of life - To your ego, or to your true self. Be true to yourself. Without it you are nothing of any substance, because the ego is nothing more than irrational fears. Nothing more than scary shadows on a wall to a child.

CHAPTER TWENTY ONE

EPILOGUE

Oaklyn Smith, forever young

On the 21st May 2011 my grandson Oaklyn was born. He passed away just seven days later. We had wet the baby's head on the day he was born, although there had been complications. I had been at the football watching my two sons and son-in-law (Jason) play for the same team, Clayton FC. A call from my daughter Kelly told us she hadn't felt the baby move for a while and was on her way to the hospital to get it checked out. The second call was to tell us she would be having an emergency caesarean and to pull Jason off the field of play. We knew by the reaction of the hospital staff that all was not well when we arrived. We got to meet Oaklyn before he was rushed away to the Royal Children's Hospital in an ambulance with his father in tow still dressed in his football gear. Mid-way through the week we heard the news no-one wanted to hear. The MRI scans indicated massive brain damage. We found out later it was due to an infection contracted while he was still in the womb. I rushed to Kelly's side. She told me on that day that she had always thought there was a meaning behind everything, but that she could see no meaning in this. I was also at a loss to see any meaning in it. A decision had to be made as to when to turn the life support off. Oaklyn's brothers, Bailey and Brody and their sister Ayrlee had grown quite attached to their new baby brother, just as we all had. On the days leading up to his last day with us, Kelly said another thing that would stick in my mind. She said she was so afraid he would be forgotten: as though he had never been here.

I can't thank the Melbourne Children's Hospital and the hospital staff enough for making his last moments with us so dignified and graceful. As I held him in my arms, after he had passed, I thought to myself; 'What purpose in this little man? Only you can know.'

Over the next few days, I recalled my experience in meditation where I experienced a knowing that there was purpose behind it all. But the knowing had been lost when I returned from that experience. It was then that a story heard years ago and long forgotten popped into my head. I don't even know where I read or heard it. It goes something like this.

All the little souls in heaven were sitting around God and one little soul said: 'God, I have never experienced forgiveness. Everyone in heaven is so kind and loving and caring there is nothing to forgive.'

God looked on the little soul and said: 'Little soul, forgiveness is a lesson, and you can only experience forgiveness in the earthly realm - the realm of suffering. But you would need another little soul to go with you to teach you this lesson.'

Another little soul spoke up. 'God, I will go to the earthly realm to help my brother learn this lesson.' But then he looked at the other little soul and said: 'Remember who I am as I strike you down, because if you forget that I am your teacher and don't forgive me, we will be stuck together in the realm of suffering until the lesson is learned.'

I thought it interesting that this story forgotten so long ago would pop into my head. But what could I get from this? Was Oaklyn just a perfect little soul with no lessons to learn? It's a comforting thought, whether true or not. Was his being here to offer us lessons? Well I suppose we all must find our own lessons from experiences like this. I thought to

152

myself: 'Have I been too quick to anger and too slow to forgive?' Sadly I had to admit I had. I still had an ego that liked to hold grudges. I let them go in that moment. This lesson of forgiveness was now learned; forgiveness frees the forgiver as well as the one forgiven. Now the second thing that popped into my head was that life is too short, be it seven days or seventy years - too short for those of us left behind. We take for granted the time we have in our relationships, often making mountains out of molehills and not cherishing the time we have together. One day will be our last day together. Will it end in harsh words or love and kindness? If you knew tomorrow would be your last day, what would you do differently today?

Later in the week, I played golf with two friends, Stuart and Kenny. We started on the practice range and most of the balls were flying down the path we wanted them to go. Then we hit the first tee. Stuart topped the ball and it went off to the left barely any distance at all. Kenny sliced off to the right beneath some trees. Both had plenty to say about this in their frustration and my shot fared no better. I smiled to myself and thought that golf could be a metaphor for relationships. Sometimes we get frustrated when people don't follow the path we would like them to take - when they behave in ways we don't like; ways we can't control. I realised then that everyone has their own path to take: their own lessons to learn. I decided to respect the path people take. Who's to know if there is a higher intelligence behind it all and there isn't some perfection to this evolution? I might have lost any real knowing of this but I can respect my experience of it. And if it leads me to an acceptance and allowance of things, it leads to me being happier.

I have no family in Australia apart from my children and grandchildren. At a funeral you often see people getting up and talking about the happy memories of the ones that have passed, and in doing so, give life again to that person. I decided to give voice to Oaklyn that day. Although he never said a word, he had spoken volumes to me since his passing. As I stood up to speak I looked at the crowded room with hundreds of our friends and family. I realised then how much love and compassion Oaklyn had managed to bring into the world already - how many hearts he had touched during his short stay. I also realised just how fortunate I was to have these people in my life. I mentioned the things above in my talk and I finished it by saying: 'I had thought I would be holding Oaklyn's hand and leading him through life. It turns out he is holding mine and leading me through my life. I found great purpose in Oaklyn being here and he will not be forgotten. I am a better man for his being here.'

Oaklyn being there was the catalyst to writing this book. Without Oaklyn being there I may never have started or finished this book. He moves my life still and to him it is dedicated, forever young in our hearts and my greatest teacher.

Life is like a roller coaster, a journey full of ups and downs, twists and turns. Hold on and enjoy the ride for it will be over too soon. Don't be afraid to get onto the roller coaster ride because you have no choice - you are already on it. Turn your apprehension to exhilaration and enjoy the ride. A successful person is a happy person. Don't believe a word I say. Test it for yourself – and in the words of that great philosopher, 'Spock' from *Star Trek*. Live long and prosper!

To my daughter Kelly, my son in law Jason and both our families I say this: *Your strength, grace and dignity, continues to amaze me. Never doubt that there was great meaning in Oaklyn being here. He will never be forgotten because he moves us still.*

ABOUT THE AUTHOR

Anthony Gilmour is a psychotherapist who specialises in anxiety and depression. His book, *TRAGIC to MAGIC,* never wavers from the point that our ultimate goal is happiness. The lessons in this book are simple, easy to understand and use. They are born of his studies and successful practice in psychotherapy over the past ten years. He also goes under the shortened name of Tony Gilmour.

Prior to becoming a psychotherapist, Tony was the CEO of a substantial engineering company. But he wasn't happy within himself. He resigned at the pinnacle of his career and began a journey of self-discovery, resulting in his highly successful career as a psychotherapist. Tony is widely read and his eclectic approach coupled with substantial clinical and business experience places him in a unique position to write this roadmap to happiness. Tony is also a qualified supervisor to other psychotherapist on case management and ethical behaviour.

What's the book about? Let's keep it simple, like the book.

Tony Gilmour takes complex theories and turns them into something so simple that most people will say it is just common sense. (But common sense is not that common!)

Tony runs a private practice in Dandenong, Victoria, Australia, and uses CD's to compliment his therapy. MP3 recordings of his programs can be downloaded from the products page at: www.melbournehypnosis.net.au.

Suggested programs to reinforce change are: Psychology of Success and Personal transformations.

Contact: info@wholemindstrategies.com.au

www.ingramcontent.com/pod-product-compliance
Lightning Source LLC
Chambersburg PA
CBHW052344090426
42739CB00011B/2306

9 780975 676288